987415

THE WORLD OF

ART

JACQUELINE DINEEN
AND
NICOLA BARBER

SILVER BURDETT PRESS
PARSIPPANY, NEW JERSEY

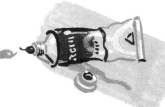

First published in the U.K. in 1997 by
Evans Brothers Limited
2A Portman Mansions
Chiltern Street
London W1M 1LE

Editor: Nicola Barber
Designer: Neil Sayer
Picture research: Victoria Brooker
Production: Jenny Mulvanny
Artwork: Anthony Jackson-Moore
Consultants: Glyn Williams, Professor of Sculpture, Royal College of Art;
Jill Kerr, Head of Art, Marple Hall School

First published in the United States in 1998 by

Silver Burdett Press Silver Burdett Press
Parsippany, NJ
A Division of Simon and Schuster
299 Jefferson Road
Parsippany, NJ 07054

Library of Congress Cataloging-in-Publication Data
Barber, Nicola.
The world of art/by Nicola Barber and Mary Mure.
p.   cm.
"First published in the U.K. in 1997 by Evans Brothers
Limited . . . London"—T. p. verso.
Includes index.
Summary: Introduces different art forms such as crafts, photography,
sculpture, painting and their materials, as
well as a brief history of art from the first cave paintings
to contemporary art of the 1990s.
1. Art—History—Juvenile literature. 2. Artists' materials—Juvenile
literature. [1. Art—History. 2. Artists' materials.
3. Art appreciation.] I. Mure, Mary. II. Title.
N5308.B36   1998   97.20487
709—dc21   CIP   AC

ISBN 0-382-39812-2 (LSB)   10 9 8 7 6 5 4 3 2 1
ISBN 0-382-39811-4 (pbk)   10 9 8 7 6 5 4 3 2 1

Printed in Spain, by GRAFO, S.A.- Bilbao

ACKNOWLEDGMENTS

For permission to reproduce copyright material, the Authors and Publishers gratefully acknowledge the following:
Cover (top left) e.t. archive (top right) Musée D'Orsay, Paris/Giraudon/Bridgeman Art Library (bottom left) Werner Forman (bottom right) © Alan Bowness, Hepworth Estate/Bridgeman Art Library **Back cover** Werner Forman**Title page** Vatican Museums and Galleries, Rome/Visual Arts Library **page 8** (top) Artephot/Kumasegawa/Visual Arts Library (bottom) e.t.archive **page 9** (top) e.t. archive (bottom) National Museum of Wales, Bridgeman Art Library **page 10** (left) e.t.archive (right) Robert Harding Picture Library **page 12** e.t.archive **page 13** Andrea Pistolesi/Image Bank **page 14** Richard Ashworth/Robert Harding Picture Library **page 15** Contarelli Chapel, S. Luigi Dei Francesi, Rome/Bridgeman Art Library **page 16, 17 and 19** e.t. archive **page 20** (top) British Museum, London/Werner Forman Archive (bottom) e.t.archive **page 21** Foto World 1991/Image Bank (bottom) e.t.archive **page 22** (top) e.t. archive (bottom) Villa dei Misteri, Pompeii/Bridgeman Art Library **page 23** e.t. archive **page 24** A. Woolfitt/Robert Harding Picture Library **page 25** Jane Taylor/Sonia Halliday Photographs **page 26** (top and bottom) e.t. archive **page 27** Vandermarst/Robert Harding Picture Library **page 28** Louvre, Paris/Bridgeman Art Library **page 29** Vatican Museums and Galleries, Rome/Bridgeman Art Library **page 30** e.t. archive **page 31** (top) e.t. archive (bottom) Kunsthistorisches Museum, Vienna/Bridgeman Art Library **page 32** Ken Takase/Artephot/Visual Arts Library **page 33** e.t. archive page 34 (left) Prado, Madrid/Bridgeman Art Library (right) Kenwood House, London/Bridgeman Art Library **page 35** Metropolitan Museum of Art, New York/Bridgeman Art Library **page 36** (top and bottom) e.t. archive **page 37** Musées Royaux des Beaux-Arts de Belgique, Brussels/Bridgeman Art Library **page 38** Philadelphia Museum of Art:George W. Elkins Collection, USA **page 39** e.t. archive **page 40** (top) Wallace Collection, London/Bridgeman Art Library (bottom) Musée D'Orsay, Paris, France/Giraudon/Bridgeman Art Library **page 41 and 42** e.t. archive **page 43** Musée D'Orsay, Paris/Giraudon/Bridgeman Art Library **page 45** *Red Interior* by Henri Matisse © Succession H Matisse/DACS 1997. e.t. archive **page 46** *Composition 8* by Wassily Kadinsky/e.t. archive **page 47** © Succession Picasso/DACS 1997. Museum of Modern Art, New York/Superstock **page 48** *Only One 1959* by Georgia O'Keeffe. National Museum of American Art, Smithsonian Institute/Bridgeman Art Library **page 49** (top) © ADAGP, Paris and DACS, London 1997. Private Collection/Bridgeman Art Library (bottom) © DEMART PRO ARTE BV/DACS 1997. Salvador Dali Museum, St. Petersburg, Florida/Bridgeman Art Library **page 50** *Blue Poles* by Jackson Pollock. Visual Arts Library **page 51** (top) © Roy Lichtenstein/DACS 1997. e.t. archive (bottom) © ARS, NY and DACS, London 1997. e.t. archive **page 52** Private Collection **page 53** (top) e.t. archive (bottom) Ontanon Nunez/Image Bank **page 54** Idemitsu Museum of Arts, Tokyo/Werner Forman Archive **page 55** (top) National Museum, Lagos, Nigeria/Werner Forman Archive (bottom) Image Bank **page 56** (top) Victoria & Albert Museum, London/Bridgeman Art Library (bottom) Sotheby's, London/Bridgeman Art Library **page 57** Copyright British Museum **page 58** (top) Werner Forman Archive/Courtesy Entwistle Gallery, London (bottom) Werner Forman Archive **page 59** (top) Flip Chalfant/Image Bank (bottom) Robert Harding Picture Library **page 60** (left) Wendy Chan/Image Bank (right) Victoria & Albert Museum, London/Bridgeman Art Library **page 61** JHC Wilson/Robert Harding Picture Library **page 62** Werner Forman Archive **page 63** (top left) e.t. archive (bottom right) Werner Forman Archive/British Museum, London **page 64** (top and bottom) Robert Harding Picture Library **page 65** Museo delle Terme, Rome/Visual Arts Library **page 66** Robert Harding Picture Library **page 67** (top) Adam Woolfitt/Robert Harding Picture Library (bottom) Sonia Halliday Photographs **page 68** (top) Vatican Museums and Galleries, Rome/Visual Arts Library (bottom) Rome Ste Marie de la Victoire/Visual Arts Library **page 69** Musée Rodin, Paris/Bridgeman Art Library **page 70** (top) *The Kiss* 1925 by Constanti Brancusi. Musée National D'Art Moderne, Paris/Lauros-Giraudon/Bridgeman Art Library (middle) Sculptures by Alexander Calder. e.t. archive (bottom) Henry Moore Foundation **page 71** © Alan Bowness, Hepworth Estate/Bridgeman Art Library **page 72** (top) e.t archive (bottom) Royal Photographic Society Picture Library **page 73** Royal Photographic Society Picture Library **page 74** e.t. archive **page 75** Royal Photographic Society Picture Library **page 76** (top) Royal Photographic Society Picture Library (bottom) Superstock **page 77** Royal Photographic Society Picture Library **page 78** Neil Tingle/Action Plus **page 79** © David Hockney 1982 **page 80** David Kemp **page 81** Jon Bradley/Rex Features **page 82** The Saatchi Collection, London **page 83** The Lisson Gallery, London **page 87** e.t archive **page 89** Musée D'Orsay, Paris/Giraudon/Bridgeman Art Library

CONTENTS

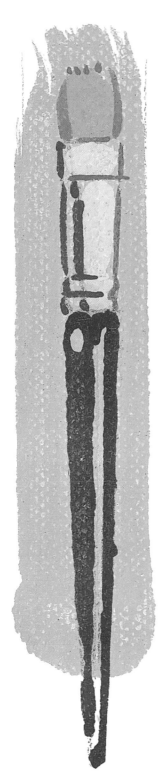

INTRODUCTION

This book is divided into six chapters. In the first chapter you can find out about the materials that artists use, how the first paints were made, and who invented the earliest brushes. You can also see how artists from all over the world use color, light, shape, and texture in their work.

Chapter two tells the story of Western art, beginning with the very first cave paintings. You can find out about some famous and some less well-known artists from the Medieval and Renaissance periods to the 20th century.

Chapter three looks at crafts from all over the world. It tells you a bit about how crafts are made and examines their history. In chapter four, you can find out about some of the greatest sculptors. Chapter five is about photography. It looks at the development of photography from the simplest early camera to the effects photographers can create today.

Finally, in chapter six, you can find out about some of the developments in art in the 1990s.

Although this book is divided into sections that deal with different aspects of art, many of these areas are

A head of the Buddha, sculpted in India in about the 5th century A.D. (see page 66)

A detail from a patterned mosaic, in Ravenna, Italy (see page 22)

closely linked. Throughout the book there are Connections boxes which highlight some of these links. If there are any words about art that you find difficult in this book, try looking them up in the Glossary of art terms (see pages 84-85). If you want to know about a particular artist, you can look up his or her name in the Glossary of artists (see pages 86-91).

Have fun finding out about art!

An embroidered hanging designed by William Morris (see page 62)

Woman and Child in a Garden at Bougival by Berthe Morisot. Morisot was one of the Impressionist painters, and was married to Manet's brother (see page 41)

MATERIALS AND METHODS IN PAINTING

If you want to paint a picture, you probably use ready-made paints out of a pot or a tube and a brush bought from a shop. But, for many centuries, artists had to make their own paints and brushes. In this chapter we look at how artists' materials were made in the past and how they are used today.

CONNECTIONS

Some artists continue to use paints made from natural substances. Aborigine artists working in Australia today still use the natural colors obtained from clay and charcoal, as well as more modern materials such as acrylic paint (see page 13).

A painting on bark by a modern-day Aborigine artist

PAINTS

The earliest artists made simple paints from natural substances found in the rocks and earth. They ground up small pieces of rock or earth to make a fine, colored powder. This powder is called a pigment. Then they mixed the pigment with animal fat or egg white or plant juices or sometimes even with blood! Different kinds of rock produced different colors. Red, yellow, and brown pigments came from a kind of earth called clay. Chalk produced a white pigment. Black pigment came from soot or charcoal. The first artists decorated rocks or pieces of bark or the walls of their caves with these basic paints.

A WHOLE WORLD OF COLOR

The range of colors grew wider as people discovered new ways to make pigments. Not all pigments come from rocks or earth. Indigo

Thousands of years ago, one of the earliest artists used a brown pigment to paint this horse on the wall of a cave in Lascaux, France.

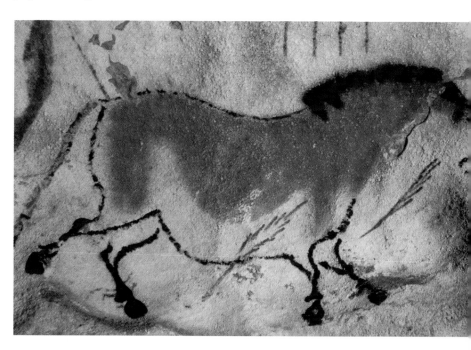

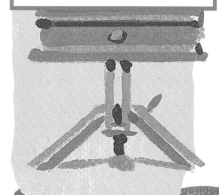

is a dark blue pigment. It comes from the leaves of the indigo plant. It was used by the Ancient Egyptians, Greeks, and Romans and by the Inca people of South America. The Ancient Greeks and Romans also used verdigris to make a bluish-green color. Verdigris forms on copper when the copper comes into contact with acid. A red pigment called carmine was made from the bodies of tiny insects called cochineal or kermes. But perhaps the most unusual way of producing a pigment was developed in India. To make the color India yellow, cattle were fed with mangoes. The mango has a soft, yellow flesh, and when the cattle urinated, their urine turned the soil yellow. People collected this soil and removed the yellow pigment from it. This practice was stopped in the late 19th century because of concerns about the health of the cattle.

In the early 18th century, the first human-made pigment was produced by a color-maker in Berlin. This pigment was made by mixing together different chemicals, and it was called Prussian blue. Today many pigments are made artificially, giving artists a whole world of colors to choose from.

BINDERS

All paints are made with pigments mixed with another substance called a binder. The binder makes the pigment into liquid paint. It helps to spread the pigment evenly, and it makes the pigment stick to the surface that is being painted. The first artists mixed their pigments with animal fats and more unusual substances (see page 10)! The Ancient Egyptians used beeswax and honey as types of binders. Until the 1400s, European artists mixed pigments with

(see page 10)

CONNECTIONS

In the late 19th century there was an explosion of color in the art world as artists began to use the new, artificial paints that had recently become available. Not only were these colors more brilliant than any pigment seen before, but they were more stable, too. This means that the paint was unlikely to change or fade over time.

PIGMENTS

In the past, pigments came from some unexpected sources:

Ultramarine: a deep blue color. It was made from a blue stone called lapis lazuli, which was mined in Afghanistan. It was highly prized and very expensive.

Red lead: an orange-red color. Made by heating lead in an oven or furnace.

Fruit stone black: black color. Made from pigments produced by burning cherry, peach, or date pits.

Brasil: a rose-pink color. Made from a kind of hardwood imported from South America. The wood was ground up to make the pigment. Artists mixed the pigment with beer, vinegar, and water to produce a paint.

Mummy: a brown color. Made from pieces taken from mummified bodies in Ancient Egypt!

egg yolks and water to make a kind of paint called egg tempera. Apprentice painters worked in the studio of a master and learned how to grind the different pigments into powder and mix them up into paints. Today artists can choose from a wide range of paints, such as oils, watercolors, gouache, poster paints, and acrylics (see box). The difference between all these kinds of paints is the binder.

THE INVENTION OF OIL PAINT

Before the 1400s most artists in Europe painted with egg tempera. The problem with egg tempera was that it dried very quickly, so painters had to be sure they did not make any mistakes. The Flemish painter Jan van Eyck (c. 1390-1441), noticed that one of his tempera paintings cracked as it dried, and he decided to try mixing the pigments with oil. He found that the new paint dried more slowly and that it did not crack. He painted it onto the canvas in thin layers, building the paint up to give more depth to the colors.

During the 15th and 16th centuries, artists discovered that oils could be used in many different ways. Instead of applying the paint in thin layers, it could be put on with thick brushstrokes so that the marks of the brush were seen in the picture. Today some artists put oil paint on with a palette knife, plastering it on thickly. Others have gone back to the method of applying thin layers.

The glowing colors in Wedding Portrait *by Jan van Eyck are a result of the artist's experiments with pigments and binders.*

APPLYING THE PAINT

The earliest people painted with simple brushes made from twigs or reeds. Sometimes they applied the paint with their hands or blew it through a tube. The Ancient Egyptians made brushes from reeds, crushing the end of the reed to make the

CONNECTIONS

Artists continue to use a wide variety of methods of applying paint. Vincent van Gogh (see page 43) sometimes used a reed pen, made from a piece of bamboo, to create pictures out of patterns of thick and thin pen strokes. The British artist Richard Long uses both hands and feet to paint some of his pictures, creating intricate patterns and bold shapes.

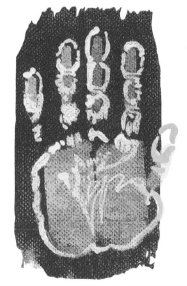

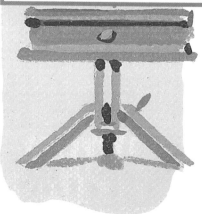

"brush" and binding the handle part with twine. Later, brushes were made from animal hair. To make hard brushes, people used hog's (pig's) hair for the bristles. The stiff bristles were bound to a stick. To make softer brushes, people used finer badger hair or sable fur pushed into the end of a quill (feather).

In China artists used the shape of the brush to create dramatic effects on the paper. Some artists even gave different kinds of brushstrokes different names, such as the "axe cut" brushstroke— a chopping, angular stroke.

Today some modern brushes have nylon bristles. Nylon bristles last longer than natural bristles. The shape of the brush is important. Flat brushes are used to put on broad areas of color. Round brushes can be shaped to a point for lines.

A modern-day Chinese artist practices painting with a fine brush.

DIFFERENT KINDS OF PAINT

Watercolors are powdered pigments combined with a kind of gum. This gum dilutes well when mixed with water. The paint is thin and transparent, so that the surface of the paper shows through the paint. Gouache and poster paints are a thicker, more dense form of watercolor. The colors dry more brightly than watercolors. **Oil paints** are pigments combined with oil. The oil is usually linseed, but poppy or walnut oil are sometimes used instead.
Pastels are sticks of color made from powdered pigments mixed with water and chalk, or oil and chalk.
Acrylic is a modern paint. The pigments are mixed with a plastic binder. Acrylic dries quickly and does not crack. Acrylic paints come in bold, bright colors and can be used on many different surfaces.

Fragments of a wall painting in Ajanta, India

PAINTING ON WALLS

Some of the earliest people painted hunting scenes on the walls of their caves. In China, people began to paint on walls about 1700 B.C., and the tradition spread to Japan and Korea. We know much about life in Ancient Egypt from the scenes painted on the walls of tombs. In Ancient Rome, houses were often decorated inside with wall paintings. This tradition was revived in southern Europe in the 1300s and 1400s to decorate churches (see page 26) by artists such as Giotto di Bondone (*c.*1266-1337) and Piero della Francesca (*c.*1420-92). The wall paintings done by these Italian artists are usually known as frescoes, because they were done while the plaster on the wall was "fresh" ("fresco"), or wet.

Fresco painting was a very skillful art. Preparing a wall to be painted took many days. Several layers of plaster were applied before a sketch of the painting was drawn onto the wall. This outline is known as a cartoon. When the artist was ready to paint, another thin layer of plaster was put over a small section of the cartoon, and the paint was applied to the wet plaster. The painting had to be done quickly, and the only way to correct a mistake was to cut out part of the plaster. The paint dried with the plaster, binding the paint into the surface of the wall itself.

CONNECTIONS

The tradition of painting on walls has continued in the 20th century, particularly in Mexico where Diego Rivera (1886-1957) and José Clemente Orozco (1883-1949) painted large scenes on the walls of public buildings during the 1930s.

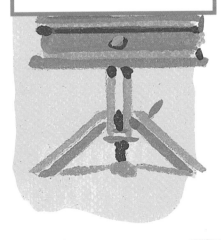

WOOD, CANVASES, AND OTHER SURFACES

The surface to which paint is applied is just as important as the paint itself. In the past the preparation of a surface often took as long as the painting! Before around 1450, most paintings were on wood. To prepare the panel, artists filled in any cracks in the wood with sawdust and glue. They covered the panel with a fine piece of linen. Then they treated the linen with several layers of plaster, called gesso, to give a fine, even painting surface.

After about 1700 most paintings were done on canvas. A canvas is a piece of linen cloth that has been stretched over a frame so that it is taut and flat to work on. After stretching, the canvas is protected with a layer of paint. Of course, artists also paint on many other surfaces including paper, board, glass, cloth, and even metal.

The Calling of St Matthew *by Michelangelo Caravaggio. The artist uses chiaroscuro (see below) to bring out the extreme drama of the scene. The shaft of sun lights up the halo and pointing hand of Christ on the right-hand side. Matthew, seated at the table, points questioningly at himself.*

The color wheel. Colors opposite each other on the wheel are called complementary colors. Reds and yellows are known as "warm" colors, while blues and greens are "cold" colors.

USING LIGHT AND COLOR

When you are painting a picture, light is very important. The way light falls can bring a scene to life and give it depth. Different kinds of light alter the appearance of colors. If light comes from above, it can make the subject look flat and dull the color. Light from the side brings out color and shape much better. Artists use the contrast of light and shadow to reveal the form, or three-dimensional shape, of an object and to create a dramatic effect. The use of light and shadow within a painting is known as chiaroscuro, from the Italian words for "clear," *chiaro* and "dark," *oscuro*.

Artists create shape by using color as well as light. The most important colors in painting are red, blue, and yellow. These are called the three primary colors of paint. Using varying mixtures of the primary colors, you can make any other color. You can see how the primary colors mix together in the color wheel (left). Colors next to each other on the color wheel go together well. Colors opposite each other on the color wheel are

known as "complementary" colors. They contrast strongly against each other. Throughout the centuries artists have used the contrasting effects of complementary colors in their paintings.

TEXTURE

Paint can be applied in different ways to give a picture texture. Many artists use various techniques to give texture to the actual surface of the painting. Some artists paint very thickly to give a rough texture. Paint put on in dabs gives a rougher texture than if it is painted on smoothly. Sometimes objects such as combs are used to make patterns in the paint. Paint can be put on with a sponge, which makes it look smudgy, or it can be flicked or dribbled over the canvas. Textured brushstrokes help to create the illusion of movement in a painting.

Mademoiselle Gachet in her garden at Auver-sur-Oise *by Vincent van Gogh. You can see the texture of the paint on the surface of this picture very clearly.*

PATTERN

A pattern is made up of a shape that is repeated several times. There are endless patterns to be found in nature, and artists frequently use patterns as the inspiration for their work. Many textile and wallpaper designs use repeating patterns (the same pattern repeated over and over again). Some patterns are made up of identical shapes that fit together perfectly. These are called tessellations. Many artists arrange the elements (color and shapes) of a picture or a sculpture to form a particular pattern. Paintings that do not have a "recognizable" subject, but use the arrangement of certain lines, patterns, color, and shapes, are known as "abstract" works of art.

A patterned mosaic of stars on a blue background from Ravenna, Italy

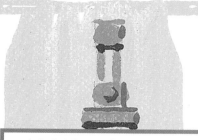

CONNECTIONS

Henri Matisse (see page 44) used the natural patterns of leaves or of a snail's shell as inspiration for his paper cutouts. He simplified the shapes and often made use of unexpected combinations of colors.

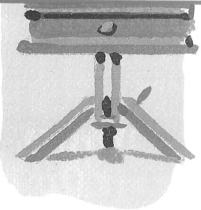

SPACE

Artists use a technique called perspective to create the idea of space in a picture. Perspective is a type of optical illusion. It relies on the fact that the farther away an object is from you, the smaller it looks. If an artist paints one large figure and one smaller figure, your eye will interpret this to mean that the smaller figure is farther away than the larger figure. Although you know that the figures are painted onto a flat piece of paper, your eye still sees depth in the picture. The first people to make a full scientific study of perspective were the artists of the Italian Renaissance (see page 27).

The Annunciation with St Emidius *by Carlo Crivelli. This painting makes full use of perspective to give an illusion of great depth. Compare the size of the figures in the foreground and background of the picture.*

ART IN THE ANCIENT WORLD

ART EVENTS	WORLD EVENTS
CIRCA **30,000** B.C.	
Earliest art known in Europe	**Old Stone Age in Europe (Upper Paleolithic) period**
CIRCA **4000** B.C.	
Gold and silver produced in Sumer.	**Sumerians rule in Mesopotamia.**
CIRCA **3000** B.C.	
Egyptian art produced for tombs and temples.	**The first pharaoh, Menes, rules in Egypt.**
CIRCA **2000** B.C.	
Assyrian art records victories in battle.	**Assyrians begin to build an empire.**
Minoan wall paintings and crafts	**Minoans settle on Crete.**
753 B.C.	
	Traditional date of founding of Rome
CIRCA **500** B.C.	
Greek sculpture at its peak	**Greek Classical period begins.**
323 B.C.	
	Alexander the Great dies.
264 B.C.	
	First Punic War between Rome and Carthage. Rome begins to expand empire.
100 B.C.	
Romans take Greek works of art.	**Roman Empire becomes more powerful as Greek civilization declines.**
A.D. **79**	
	Vesuvius erupts, burying Pompeii and Herculaneum.

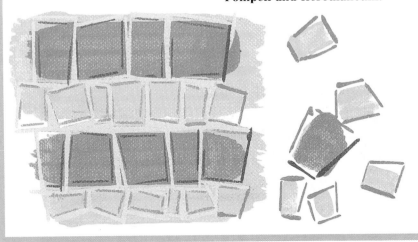

The first artists known to us were painting about 25,000 years ago. We know about these artists from paintings that have been found hidden away, deep inside caves. We can be certain that people were painting and drawing before this time, and that they painted not only on cave walls, but no other examples have survived. The most famous early cave paintings are in France, at Lascaux, and in Spain, at Altamira. The cave walls are covered in pictures of animals—bison, deer, horses, reindeer, and mammoths. Early people hunted these animals for food. It is likely that these pictures were part of a magic ceremony, performed to make sure that the hunt was successful and that people would not go hungry.

The people who painted the cave paintings were hunters and gatherers. This means that they moved around from place to place, hunting animals and gathering plants. But between about 12,000 and 7,000 years ago, people began to settle in one place. This was possible because they had learned to domesticate some animals and to cultivate some plants for crops. The animals and crops provided a reliable source of food, and the human population increased. People began to have more free time, and crafts such as pottery and weaving

developed (you can find out more about crafts on pages 53-63).
Some people started to specialize in different crafts.

THE ART OF ANCIENT EGYPT

The great early civilizations began to develop from this settled way of life. The civilization of Ancient Egypt lasted about 3,000 years, from around 3000 B.C. to 30 B.C. Nearly all Egyptian art was concerned with religion. For those who could afford it, it was important to prepare for life after death. The Egyptian pharaohs (kings) built huge tombs, many in the shape of pyramids. Nobles from the royal household had tombs grouped around the pharaoh's pyramid. The walls of these tombs, and of other buildings such as temples, were covered with paintings of everyday life and of battle scenes. Much of what we know about life in Ancient Egypt comes from the evidence of these paintings.

ART IN MESOPOTAMIA

We know a lot about the art of the Ancient Egyptians from the evidence left behind in tombs and other remains. But Ancient Egypt was not the only flourishing civilization of the time. In the valley between the Tigris and Euphrates rivers, in present-day

DRAWING IN STYLE

Artists in Ancient Egypt followed strict rules in their drawings. They drew different parts of the human body from the most characteristic angle. It was easier for artists to draw a face looking sideways, but they showed the eye as if you were looking from the front. The top half of the body was seen from the front so that both arms were balanced, but legs were drawn from the side, in profile.

An Egyptian wall painting showing a nobleman, his wife, and daughter catching birds in the marshes of the Nile River

Iraq, was a region called Mesopotamia. The first civilization to grow up in Mesopotamia was that of the Sumerians. The Sumerians ruled from the city of Ur from about 4000 B.C. Like the Egyptians, Sumerian kings and queens were buried with great ceremony, in preparation for life in the next world. When the royal burial ground at Ur was excavated in 1922, gold and silver jewelry and headdresses were found, as well as gold and silver vessels and ornaments, a gold helmet, and even a harp decorated with animals.

Other civilizations followed in Mesopotamia. The Assyrians, who were ruthless warriors, broke away from the Sumerians in about 2,000 B.C. and began to build a mighty empire. Much of Assyrian art records Assyrian victories in battle. Many of these records were in the form of stone relief (see page 64) carvings on buildings.

THE ART OF THE CLASSICAL WORLD

Greek art began on the island of Crete where people settled and built up a civilization in about 2,000 B.C. These people are called the Minoans, after a king in Ancient Greek legend. They

Gold headdress, earrings and necklaces found in the royal burial ground at Ur, Mesopotamia

A relief carving from the royal palace in Nineveh showing an Assyrian king in his war-chariot

One of the wall paintings from the Minoan palace of Knossos

were named by the British archaeologist, Sir Arthur Evans, who first studied Minoan civilization.

In 1900, Sir Arthur Evans discovered a magnificent palace at Knossos in Crete. From the ruins of this palace, it became clear that the Minoans were talented artists. They decorated the walls of Knossos and of their other palaces with beautiful wall paintings. They also produced exquisite craft work—ivory work, jewelry, and bronze ornaments have all been found on the island.

The greatest time for Greek art is known as the Classical Period. It began in about 500 B.C. The most impressive achievements were in the field of sculpture (see page 65). The Greeks also developed their own styles of painting. Unfortunately, we do not know much about Greek painters except for their pictures on pottery. The Greeks decorated a range of pots, jars, bowls, and cups, all usually known as "vases," with red or black figures in scenes from everyday life as well as from myths and legends. Vase painting built up into a thriving industry in Athens, one of the most powerful city-states in Greece, in the 6th century B.C. Compared to Egyptian styles of painting (see page 19) the figures on these vases are painted in a much more realistic way, with all of the body seen

CONNECTIONS

Greek artists used a technique of perspective (see page 17) called "foreshortening" to make their figures look realistic. For example, a foot looks shorter from the front than it does from the side, and so the Greeks painted it like that. This was a great leap forward in artistic technique.

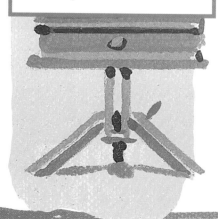

An Ancient Greek vase showing philosophers in conversation

A beautiful Roman mosaic showing an actor playing the tambourine

from one angle and fine details of the way clothes fall and drape.

THE ROMAN INFLUENCE

By tradition, the city of Rome was founded in 753 B.C. By the 1st century B.C. the Romans had conquered much of Western Europe and the Mediterranean, including the lands of the Greeks. The Romans took Greek works of art to Rome and copied their style. They also employed Greek craft workers. One technique that was borrowed from the Greeks and developed by the Romans was the art of mosaic. Mosaics are made from small pieces, called "tesserae," of colored stone or tile. These pieces were set into a type of cement to make patterns and pictures to cover floors and sometimes walls.

A wall painting from a house in Pompeii. It shows a servant pouring liquid from a jug.

ARTISTS IN POMPEII

Not much Roman painting has survived, but some of the finest examples have been preserved thanks to a volcano! The towns of Pompeii and Herculaneum were wiped out by the eruption of the volcano, Vesuvius, in A.D. 79. The towns were covered in volcanic ash and mud. When the ruins were excavated, centuries later, archaeologists found buildings decorated with mosaics and beautiful wall paintings. These remains have given us valuable evidence about art in the Roman Empire.

MEDIEVAL AND RENAISSANCE ART

ART EVENTS	WORLD EVENTS
	A.D. 300 4TH CENTURY
	Emperor Constantine makes Christianity the official religion of Roman Empire (313).
	Constantinople becomes new capital of Roman Empire (330).
	400 5TH CENTURY
Celts and other nomadic peoples develop their own art in Europe.	The fall of Rome. The so-called "Dark Ages" begin (476).
	500 6TH CENTURY
Hagia Sophia built in Constantinople by Emperor Justinian (532-7).	"Barbarian" kingdoms established in Europe.
	1000 11TH CENTURY
The building of great European churches begins.	William the Conqueror becomes king of England after the Battle of Hastings (1066).
Norman and Romanesque architecture	
	First Crusade (1095-9)
	1100 12TH CENTURY
Building of Notre Dame Cathedral in Paris begins (1163)	
Gothic architecture	
	1200 13TH CENTURY
Cimabue and Giotto begin to paint church frescoes.	Signing of Magna Carta in England (1215)
	1400 15TH CENTURY
The Renaissance begins in Florence.	Wars of Roses in England (1455-85)
Brunelleschi, Donatello, Masaccio at work	Columbus sails for America (1492).
	1500 16TH CENTURY
Leonardo da Vinci paints *Mona Lisa* (c. 1503).	Luther demands reform of Roman Catholic Church. (1517)
Michelangelo begins work on ceiling of Sistine Chapel (1508).	Reformation begins in Europe.
Hans Holbein, Pieter Bruegel the Elder among northern painters of the time	
El Greco settles in Spain. (1577)	

NEW INFLUENCES

After the fall of the Roman Empire in A.D. 476, Europe was the scene of many migrations and battles. Groups of Celts, Franks, Angles, Saxons, and Jutes all moved and settled in new lands. This period is often called the Dark Ages because people once considered it to be a time of confusion, when little art of any note was produced.

The exquisite silver and gold helmet from the Sutton Hoo treasure, found in eastern Britain. This helmet was made by the Anglo-Saxon people in about the 7th century A.D.

Inside Hagia Sophia, Istanbul, Turkey. This huge domed building was constructed over 1400 years ago.

CONNECTIONS

Like the Romans, Byzantine artists were very skilled at making mosaics. The massive dome inside Hagia Sophia was originally covered with gold, silver, and glass mosaics, which glittered in the sunlight. (These were covered over when the Turks conquered the city.) In Ravenna, Italy, a series of mosaics in the church of San Vitale show the Emperor Justinian himself with his wife, Theodora, and their servants.

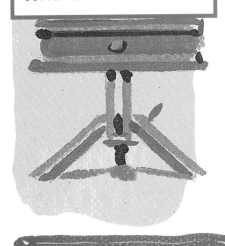

In fact, all these peoples had their own rich artistic traditions, often producing intricately decorated ornaments, jewelry, and weapons.

The other great influence on life and on art during this time was the spread of Christianity across Europe. In the early days of Christianity, the Romans persecuted Christians for their beliefs. But in A.D. 313, the Emperor Constantine made Christianity an official religion of the Roman Empire. Churches were built, and as time went by, more and more people were converted to Christianity.

In A.D. 330, the city of Byzantium (now Istanbul in Turkey) became the new capital of the Roman Empire. It was renamed Constantinople after the Emperor Constantine. After the fall of Rome in 476, Constantinople became the center of what was to become the Byzantine Empire. Some magnificent churches were built in the city, the most famous being Hagia Sophia, the Church of Holy Wisdom, which was built in A.D. 532-7 by the Emperor

ILLUMINATED MANUSCRIPTS

In Christian monasteries in Ireland and England, monks produced illuminated manuscripts. These were handwritten copies of the Bible and other religious works, beautifully decorated with ink and paint, and even more expensive materials such as gold and silver leaf. Some examples of these books, such as *The Book of Kells* and the *Lindisfarne Gospels*, have survived to this day.

Inside Durham Cathedral, Britain. You can see the massive round arches along the side, and the skeleton of thinner ribs running across the roof.

Justinian. This building still stands today as an awe-inspiring example of Byzantine art. The church was turned into a mosque by the Turks who conquered the city in the 15th century.

CHURCHES AND CATHEDRALS

During the 11th century, work began on some of the great cathedrals of Europe. These new buildings were made of stone, with massive round arches. This style of architecture is called Romanesque, named after its round, Roman-style arches.

In Britain, Durham Cathedral is a fine example of Romanesque architecture. It has sturdy, round arches, but its architect came up with an ingenious idea to make the roof less heavy. The roof has a skeleton of thin ribs. In between the ribs, the roof is filled in with a thin stone skin. This idea was developed in the following centuries to create a new style of architecture, known as Gothic. Gothic architecture used pointed arches instead of round ones. These pointed arches and ribbed ceilings (called ribbed vaults) allowed Gothic cathedrals to be built higher and higher. In fact, part of the cathedral at Beauvais in northern France was built so high (about 150 feet) that the roof eventually collapsed!

PAINTING ON GLASS

Gothic cathedrals were designed to have large windows, and these windows were filled with colored glass, called stained glass. Most of the earliest surviving stained glass dates from the 12th and 13th centuries, although the method of setting colored glass into a metal frame was already in use before this date. Large sheets of glass were fired in a particular color. These sheets were then cut to the required shapes. Often details were painted onto the glass in different colors.

One of the scenes from the life of Christ painted by Giotto di Bondone in the Scrovegni Chapel, Padua, Italy. This scene shows the flight of Mary, Joseph, and the baby Jesus into Egypt.

Madonna Enthroned *by Cimabue*

GIOTTO

While some churches were decorated with mosaics, or with stunning stained glass, many artists in Italy were employed to paint the walls of churches. These paintings are called frescoes (see page 14). The art of painting walls had largely died out after the end of the Roman Empire, but it was revived by Cimabue (*c.*1240-1302) and Giotto di Bondone. Cimabue worked at Assisi and in Florence. His frescoes and paintings are done in bright, jewel-like colors. Giotto's colors were more muted, and his approach to painting figures was quite new. Giotto painted the people in his scenes as if they were based on living models. He tried to make a scene look natural and realistic. He cut out any fussy details and made his paintings strong and simple, concentrating attention on the rounded figures themselves. Giotto worked mainly in Florence, but his fame soon spread far and wide.

THE REBIRTH OF CLASSICAL ART

During the 15th century, people began to challenge the ideas handed down from the previous thousand years and to develop new ideas of their own. This change started in Italy where people

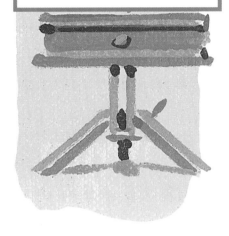

became interested in Ancient Greek and Roman art and culture and wanted to revive it. This was because sculpture and artifacts from Ancient Greece and Rome were being rediscovered, creating a fascination for these great ancient cultures. This period in European history is called the Renaissance.

The Renaissance began in Florence, where wealthy merchants and bankers began to sponsor artists. This gave artists more freedom because it meant that they did not have to rely on church commissions to make money. Florence's leading family, the de' Medici, were powerful bankers who took a great interest in the arts and spent a great deal of money on making Florence an artistic center that became famous throughout Europe.

PAINTERS AND PERSPECTIVE

Painters were influenced by Giotto's work and by the new interest in Classical art. The first artists to study the human body closely in order to produce accurate and realistic work were sculptors such as Donatello (see page 67). Another step forward was the use of perspective to give an illusion of distance (see page 17). The first painter to make use of perspective was Masaccio (1401-28), in a wall painting for a church in Florence. This is called *The Holy Trinity with the Virgin and St. John*. The perspective of the picture makes it look as though Christ, Mary, and St. John are set into a recess in the wall, with a merchant and his wife kneeling outside.

The city of Florence in northern Italy, as it looks today

FILIPPO BRUNELLESCHI

The leader of the young Florentine artists who began the Renaissance was Filippo Brunelleschi (1377–1446), a sculptor and architect. He was commissioned to complete the magnificent cathedral in Florence. The people of the city wanted the cathedral to be topped by a huge dome resting on pillars—but no one knew how to achieve this. Brunelleschi designed a dome by studying the ruins of ancient buildings in Rome. His ideas were to be followed by architects for the next 500 years. Brunelleschi was famous for another development in art. He introduced a method for working out perspective. The first painter to use this method was Masaccio (see page 27).

*Leonardo da Vinci's most famous painting,
the* Mona Lisa

LEONARDO DA VINCI

One of the best-known artists of the Italian Renaissance is Leonardo da Vinci (1452-1519). Leonardo was interested in everything in the world around him. He examined plants with a magnifying glass to see how they grew and changed. He watched storms and studied the flight of insects and birds. He cut up several dead human bodies in order to learn more about human anatomy, and he filled sketchbooks with drawings and notes about his discoveries.

Leonardo spent his life drawing, painting, and sculpting, but sometimes did not complete a painting. Unfortunately, the works that he did complete and that survive today are mostly in a bad condition. However, even from these examples we can see how Leonardo's painting was different from the work of other artists.

One of Leonardo's most famous paintings is the *Mona Lisa*. It is a portrait of a Florentine lady called Lisa. She appears to look out of the picture with a sad, wistful expression. Leonardo painted in oils and developed a technique of blending and blurring the colors together, called *sfumato*. This blurring means that there are no definite outlines in the picture. Instead Leonardo used the contrasts of light and dark (chiaroscuro: see page 15) to model the face. This is partly what gives the *Mona Lisa* her celebrated, "mysterious" look.

Looking up at the ceiling of the Sistine Chapel in the Vatican, Rome, Italy. The ceiling was painted by Michelangelo between 1508 and 1512.

Michelangelo Buonarroti

Another important Renaissance artist was the painter and sculptor Michelangelo Buonarroti (1475-1564). One of Michelangelo's most extraordinary works is the ceiling of the Sistine Chapel in Rome.

In 1506, Michelangelo received a message from Pope Julius II in Rome. The Pope wanted Michelangelo to carve a magnificent tomb for him. Michelangelo was excited at the prospect. He planned a massive structure with huge sculpted figures, and he went to Carrara to choose marble for the tomb. When Michelangelo returned to Rome and started work, he found that the Pope was having second thoughts about the tomb. Instead, the Pope commissioned Michelangelo to paint the ceiling of the Sistine Chapel in the Vatican. Michelangelo lay on his back on scaffolding to paint the ceiling of the chapel. It took him four years to complete the work. When he had finished it, Michelangelo went back to his favorite art form—sculpture (see page 68).

A self-portrait by Albrecht Dürer, painted in 1498. Dürer was one of the first painters to paint his own portrait.

THE RENAISSANCE IN NORTHERN EUROPE

The 15th century was a very prosperous time in northern Europe. Wealthy merchants could afford to commission paintings and this gave artists the chance to experiment with their style of painting.

One of the best-known of the early northern Renaissance artists was the Flemish painter Jan van Eyck (see page 12). Van Eyck painted portraits and scenes of people set in everyday settings, as well as religious scenes. Van Eyck used perspective in his pictures. His use of oils gave his pictures a warmth and liveliness not seen in tempera paintings.

Other artists began to travel further afield in their search for new ideas and techniques. The German artist Albrecht Dürer (1471-1528), was the son of a goldsmith. He was brought up in Nuremberg, and even as a boy he was a gifted artist. He became an apprentice in a workshop producing altars and woodcuts, and then traveled to Italy to study the work of the Italian masters. When he returned to Nuremberg, he had absorbed a great deal of knowledge, which he combined with his training in German art. His talent and imagination made him a driving force in introducing Renaissance ideas into northern Europe.

THE REFORMATION

By the end of the 15th century, the Roman Catholic Church had become very powerful throughout Europe. Some people criticized the wealth and power of the Church. In 1517, a German monk called Martin Luther demanded reform, and helped to begin a movement called the Reformation. This led to the establishment of Protestant Churches.

EVIL AND DEMONS

One of the strangest artists of the early 16th century was Hieronymus Bosch (c.1450-1516). We know hardly anything about Bosch except that he lived in Holland and died in 1516, but he became famous for his terrifying pictures illustrating the evil in humans and the demons that punish sinners.

The Reformation had serious effects for painters in northern Europe. Many Protestants thought that religious paintings supported the Roman Catholic Church, and so painters began to lose commissions for altar panels and other church art. One painter to be affected by these changes was the German artist Hans Holbein the Younger (*c*. 1497-1543). Holbein hoped to become a leading religious painter of the German-speaking countries, but the Reformation put an end to these plans. In 1526 he went to London where he soon established himself as a portrait painter. King Henry VIII made him court painter at the English court, and Holbein painted several portraits of the King, his wives, and nobles.

Pieter Bruegel the Elder (*c*. 1525-69) was a Flemish painter who made detailed paintings of the lives of ordinary people, such as peasants working in the fields, feasting, and merrymaking. Bruegel also saw scenes of horror on his travels. In Flanders, Protestant believers wanted to break away from Spanish Catholic rule. In 1556 the new king of Spain, Philip II, tried to crush the rebels. Thousands of Flemish people were killed. Bruegel painted some of these horrific scenes.

A portrait of King Henry VIII of England by Hans Holbein. Holbein was court painter at the English court, and painted several pictures of the king, his wives, and nobles.

An everyday scene, Hunters in the Snow, *by Pieter Bruegel the Elder*

THE 17TH AND 18TH CENTURIES

ART EVENTS	WORLD EVENTS
1600 17TH CENTURY	
Rubens opens his workshop in Antwerp (1608).	The beginning of the Baroque Period (c.1600)
Velázquez appointed Court Painter to King Philip IV of Spain (1623).	Thirty Years' War in Europe (1618-48)
	Pilgrims sail to North America (1620).
Bernini begins colonnade of the Piazza of St. Peter's, Rome (1656).	Louis XIV (the Sun King) becomes King of France (1643).
Rembrandt and Vermeer painting in Netherlands	Fire of London (1666)
1700 18TH CENTURY	
Rococo style develops in France.	The start of the Georgian period in Britain when George I becomes king (1714)
	Pompeii and Herculaneum rediscovered (1748).
Start of Neoclassical Period	Industrial Revolution begins in Britain (c.1750)
Sir Joshua Reynolds founds Royal Academy in London (1768).	American Declaration of Independence (1776)
Gainsborough rivals Reynolds as portrait painter with works such as *Miss Haverfield* (1780).	
Jacques Louis David paints pictures to support French revolutionaries.	The storming of the Bastille leads to start of French Revolution (1789).
Louvre art gallery in Paris opens (1793).	

The Madeleine in Paris, an example of a building in the Neoclassical style (see page 36)

THE BAROQUE STYLE

In the middle of the 16th century, Catholic authorities tried to resist the effects of the Reformation by starting a movement called the Counter-Reformation. It was stated that Catholic art should have only one aim, which was to bring people back to the Catholic Church. By the end of the 16th century, a new style of art had begun in Rome. This style became known as the Baroque. Paintings and sculpture portrayed vivid and dramatic images of saints, miracles, and the crucifixion. This flamboyant style was used to make Catholic beliefs seem more popular to the people. By the early 17th century, Rome was once again the artistic capital of Europe, due to the patronage of Church officials and leading families.

The painter Michelangelo da Caravaggio (1573-1610), came from a village near Milan and went to Rome early in the Baroque Period. He had a wild temper and was arrested and imprisoned several times. Caravaggio was not concerned with making his paintings beautiful. He painted religious scenes as if they were part of everyday life, involving everyday people—even if they were ugly! He used dramatic contrasts of light and shade,

The lavish Baroque interior of the Church of Il Gesù, Rome, Italy

CONNECTIONS

Artemisia Gentileschi (1593-*c*.1652) was the daughter of a follower of Caravaggio. Not surprisingly, she was influenced by Caravaggio's work. She painted powerful, dramatic pictures, often showing female characters from the Bible. One of her most famous paintings is *Judith Slaying Holofernes*. This shows the moment when Judith hacks off the head of the drunken general, Holofernes, in order to save her city from defeat by the Assyrians. The picture is startlingly realistic, and like Caravaggio's paintings makes dramatic use of chiaroscuro.

highlighting the expressions on the faces of people in his paintings (see page 15). Many people were shocked by Caravaggio's violent style.

Another painter with a very individual style was known as El Greco ("the Greek") (1541-1614). His figures, with their elongated limbs and pale faces, have a ghostly look, and his colors are often lurid. His style of painting is known as Mannerism.

THE SPREAD OF BAROQUE

As the Baroque style spread from Italy to other parts of Europe it changed slightly from country to country. But it always kept its vivid images and contrasts of light and shade.

Peter Paul Rubens (1577-1640) was a Flemish painter who went to Rome in 1600, while Caravaggio was painting there. By the time Rubens returned to his home town of Antwerp, he had learned a great deal. He established his own workshop where he and his pupils painted portraits and religious and mythological scenes. Rubens had a genius for arranging large complicated compositions, which were full of movement and life.

On a visit to Spain, Rubens met another young painter, Diego Velázquez (1599-1660), who was court painter to King Philip IV in Madrid. Rubens suggested that Velázquez should visit Rome to study the work of the Italian painters. Velázquez went to

Rome in 1630 and was very impressed by Caravaggio's use of light and portrayal of people. He returned to Spain, where his job at court was to paint members of the royal family. Velázquez used light and harmony of color to bring his portraits to life, showing the sheen and texture of different materials and accurately capturing the expression on his subjects' faces.

The Maids of Honour by Diego Velázquez. Velázquez shows himself painting a portrait of the Spanish king and queen. The portrait is reflected in the mirror on the back wall. At the center of the picture is Princess Margarita surrounded by her maids.

PROTESTANT BAROQUE

Baroque art in the Netherlands was less flamboyant than in other parts of Europe. The southern part of the country (present-day Belgium) was still Catholic, but the northern region was Protestant. The Protestants believed that artists should not portray scenes from the Bible, and the wealthy merchants who commissioned artists preferred plainer styles in architecture and painting. So Dutch artists painted mostly portraits, landscapes, and interior scenes.

The finest Dutch painter of all was Rembrandt van Rijn (1606-69). He began as a portrait painter and throughout his life painted self-portraits—about 60 in all. He sometimes painted people in exotic costumes because he liked to capture the effects of the light on rich fabrics, jewelry, and swords. Though unusual in the Protestant Netherlands, Rembrandt also painted

A self-portrait by Rembrandt van Rijn, showing the artist as an old man

Young Woman with a Water Jug *by Jan Vermeer. Notice how Vermeer uses the effect of light on the shiny metal of the jug and bowl.*

many religious scenes, achieving powerful dramatic effects through the use of light and shadows.

Another Dutch painter, Jan Vermeer (1632-75), painted the interiors of Dutch houses. His pictures do not have the drama of Rembrandt's work. They are quiet and serene, and the people in them are often performing some simple task such as pouring milk into a bowl. Vermeer painted with clear, jewel-like colors, and the objects in his paintings are arranged so that the light brings out color and texture.

ROCOCO

During the first half of the 18th century, a new style of art developed in France. The court of King Louis XV liked rich, graceful decoration and found Baroque too heavy and grand. The style that developed was called Rococo. It was more refined than Baroque and fit into the elegant, highly decorated interiors of the time. The Rococo style spread throughout Europe.

NEOCLASSICAL ART

In 1748, the towns of Pompeii and Herculaneum in Italy (see page 22) were rediscovered. Scholars and scientists began to uncover the ancient towns and piece together Classical history far more accurately than they had been able to do before. This reawakened interest in Classical life and led to a new style known as Neoclassical art. Scholars and artists visited Italy and Greece and tried to recreate Classical life in their work.

A French vase in the Neoclassical style. It dates from around 1785.

In England the painter Sir Joshua Reynolds (1723-92) founded the Royal Academy of Art in London to preserve Classical ideas in art. He later became its first president. Georgian houses were modeled on Roman villas or Greek temples.

Sir Joshua Reynolds came to be in great demand among elegant London society as a portrait painter. Reynolds's chief rival was Thomas Gainsborough (1727-88). Gainsborough was a naturally gifted painter, who was largely self-taught. He did not believe that art had to be grand and impressive in the style of the great Classical works. His style was simpler than Reynolds's, and he had a gift for painting fine fabrics, delicate lace, and shining silks and capturing the likeness of his sitters.

Mrs. Siddons *by Thomas Gainsborough*

CONNECTIONS

Napoleon opened to the public a national museum and art gallery in the old royal palace of the Louvre in Paris. Today the Louvre houses a huge collection of paintings and sculptures including some very famous works such as Leonardo da Vinci's *Mona Lisa* (see page 28).

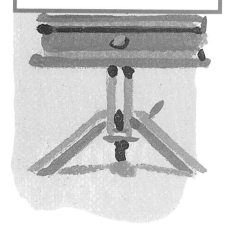

A NARROW ESCAPE

Marie-Élisabeth-Vigée-Lebrun (1755-1842) was a well-known portrait painter in France in the late 18th century. She was also a close friend of Queen Marie Antoinette. When the king and queen were arrested by the French revolutionaries, Vigée-Lebrun was forced to flee for her life. She traveled around the courts of Europe and earned enough money from her painting to live in comfort for the rest of her life.

THE FRENCH REVOLUTION

In France unrest was brewing in the late 18th century. The French king, Louis XVI, was weak, and his wife Marie Antoinette was vain and extravagant. In July 1789, the people of Paris rebelled against the aristocrats and stormed the Bastille, the large fortress prison in the heart of the city. The king and queen and about 1,500 aristocrats and antirevolutionaries were sent to the guillotine.

The painter Jacques Louis David (1748-1825) was a friend of the revolutionaries and painted pictures in support of their ideals. He portrayed their spirit of battle by painting Classical scenes of Roman heroes fighting barbarian invaders. After the Revolution, Napoleon Bonaparte began to build an empire for France. David painted many flattering portraits of the new French leader.

The Death of Marat *by Jacques Louis David. Marat was one of the leaders of the French Revolution. He was murdered in his bathtub.*

THE 19TH CENTURY

ART EVENTS	WORLD EVENTS
1800 19TH CENTURY	
Constable exhibits *The Haywain* in Paris (1824).	Napoleon becomes Emperor of France (1804).
Start of photography with Niepce and Daguerre (1827)	Stephenson's *Rocket* wins speed trials in England (1829)
Barbizon Group meets near Paris (1848).	Revolutions in Europe (1848-9)
Courbet shocks with his exhibition in Paris (1855).	
Manet and others turned down for exhibition in Paris. The outcry leads to a new exhibition, Salon for the Rejected (1863).	American Civil War (1861-5)
Monet exhibits *Impression: Sunrise*, which gives the Impressionist movement its name (1872).	Alexander Graham Bell invents telephone (1876).
	New York lit by electricity (1882).
Cézanne begins his experimental work in Aix-le-Provence (1886).	Daimler produces first "horseless carriage" (1886).
Van Gogh goes to paint in southern France (1888).	Eiffel Tower built (1889)
	Pierre and Marie Curie discover radium (1898).

One of the many paintings of Mont St Victoire, just outside Aix-en-Provence, made by the French painter Paul Cézanne (see pages 42-3)

THE AGE OF ROMANTICISM

The revolution against British rule in America beginning in 1775 was the start of great changes during the late 18th and early 19th centuries. The Americans' success helped to spark the French Revolution. A different kind of "revolution," known as the Industrial Revolution, began in Great Britain in about 1750. This was a time of new inventions, allowing goods to be mass-produced in factories. A new class of business people emerged, the powerful men who ran the industries. All these changes were reflected in the arts. In many countries court life disappeared, and there were few royal patrons to commission artists. The buyers of art were now mainly the middle classes—wealthy bankers, lawyers, and business people.

Paris became the center of the art world in the 19th century. Many artists began to rebel against the old traditions. They wanted to find new ways of expressing themselves by portraying passions and violence and, exploring the relationship between people and the natural world. Many of these artists started to record the lives of poor working people rather than paint grand Classical scenes from history or mythology.

FRANCISCO DE GOYA

Francisco de Goya (1746-1828) had a traditional role as a painter at the Spanish court. However, he painted what he saw with honesty and realism, whether his subject was the royal family or the atrocities of war. He did not flatter his royal patrons in their portraits, and when Napoleon's army occupied Spain, Goya painted dramatic pictures showing the horrific treatment of Spanish fighters by Napoleon's soldiers.

CONSTABLE AND TURNER

Two English painters influenced the work of the French artists. They were both landscape painters. In the 18th century, paintings of landscapes were usually imaginative, created to look like an ideal Italian scene. However, John Constable (1776-1837) painted nature as he saw it, with clouds and rain and shining light on water. One of Constable's paintings, *The Haywain*, was exhibited in Paris in 1824 and greatly influenced the French painters of the time. The other English artist was Joseph Mallord Turner (1775-1851), who painted dramatic pictures, often using color and swirling shapes rather than definite outlines to show storms and raging seas.

The Haywain *by John Constable*

A Wagon and Team of Horses *by Rosa Bonheur*

Jean Françóis Millet (1814-75) painted scenes from peasant life. His picture The Gleaners *shows three women hard at work in the fields. It is very different from the romantic landscapes of the past.*

THE BARBIZON GROUP

In the 1840s a group of artists met in the small town of Barbizon near Paris to paint landscapes. They were inspired by Constable's painting at the Paris exhibition. They worked in the open air so that they too could capture the effects of light on the natural landscape around them.

One of the painters in this group, Jean Baptiste Camille Corot (1796-1875) was a landscape painter who had often traveled to Italy to paint. He painted objects as areas of light and shade rather than giving them hard, definite outlines, modeling the shapes with thick brushstrokes.

This new approach to out-of-door painting inspired one of the most successful female artists of the 19th century. Rosa Bonheur (1822-99) painted animals, and was so intent on portraying her subjects accurately that she dissected dead animals to learn more about their anatomy. She was an unusual figure, with short cropped hair and often seen wearing trousers. She became famous throughout Europe and the United States, particularly for her painting *The Horse Fair*.

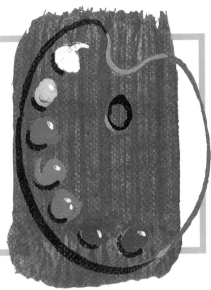

BONJOUR, MONSIEUR COURBET

In 1855 the painter Gustave Courbet (1819-77) caused a stir when he opened a one-man exhibition to display his new style, which he called Realism. Courbet wanted to show life as it really was, and he shied away from any prettiness in painting. In one of his paintings, *Bonjour, Monsieur Courbet,* he portrays himself as a shabbily dressed artist in shirtsleeves and boots, his painting gear strapped to his back, walking through the French countryside and on his way meeting two smartly dressed gentlemen.

THE IMPRESSIONISTS

A group of artists led by Édouard Manet (1832-83) were impressed by Courbet's ideas, (see box) and they set out to change the traditional rules of art, which they felt had become meaningless. In the past, artists had usually painted people in a studio, with artificial or carefully directed light. Manet and his group realized that sunlight in the open air is very different from the gradual changes of light and shade in a studio. Sunlight creates harsh contrasts, with deep shadows and bright colors. Manet painted people's faces as they appeared in bright sunlight. The features are not sharply defined, and the faces look flat, unlike the rounded faces of conventional portraits. Though these paintings may not look unusual today, they caused an outcry from the traditional art world when they first appeared in Paris.

One of the painters who joined Manet was a poor young man called Claude Monet (1840-1926). He painted in a small boat so that he could study the changing effects of light on the river. He developed a technique of painting with quick strokes, capturing a particular moment without worrying too much about the detail. This led to another departure from traditional art which caused more criticism from the art world. The study of light at different times and in different conditions also fascinated Monet. He often painted the same scene at different times of day,

Concert in the Tuileries Gardens by *Édouard Manet, one of Manet's many outdoor scenes*

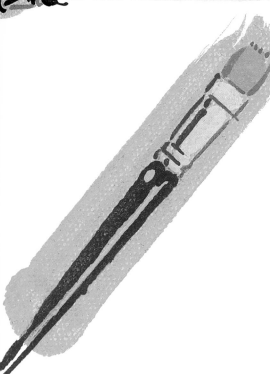

noting how the light changed.

THE INFLUENCE OF JAPAN

Another source of inspiration for the Impressionists came from Japan. Japanese prints were often used up as wrapping for imported goods from the East. Manet and his group were excited by these pictures, because they often showed only part of a subject, and did not conform to traditional European rules. One of the painters who was most affected by these prints was Edgar Degas (1834-1917). He went to ballet rehearsals and drew ballerinas from all angles. He studied the effects of foreshortening and of stage lighting on the human body. Back in his studio, he would compose his pictures, often showing only part of a figure cut off by the edge of the picture, or a figure from an unusual angle.

Mary Cassatt, (1844-1926) was another Impressionist artist who was influenced by Japanese prints. She was an American who went to Paris in 1868 to train and work with the Impressionists. She became a close friend of Degas, and settled in France for the rest of her life.

AFTER THE IMPRESSIONISTS

Paul Cézanne (1839-1906) painted with the Impressionists as a young man, but he was so disgusted by the response to their

GAUGUIN

Paul Gauguin (1848-1903) also started painting in Paris but later went to the island of Tahiti in the Pacific Ocean. Gauguin was looking for a simple way of life. He wanted to get away from the sophistication of European art and to paint in a style that showed the character of the people around him. People found his pictures very strange when he brought them back to Europe. Very disappointed with this reaction, Gauguin returned to Tahiti where he stayed for the rest of his life. Like van Gogh, he died unknown and very poor.

Four Ballerinas *by Edgar Degas. Notice how the figure on the right-hand side is cut off by the edge of the picture.*

CONNECTIONS

Cézanne is often called a Post-Impressionist (After-Impressionist) because he developed the ideas of the Impressionists. He said that he wanted to "make of Impressionism something solid and durable." He studied the structure of everyday objects such as a fruit bowl, and of outdoor scenes, and used combinations of complementary colors (see page 15) and bold brushstrokes to convey solidity and form. His methods became a very important influence for artists such as Picasso and Braque (see page 46).

Self-portrait by Vincent van Gogh, painted in 1889. You can see the heavy brushstrokes running through the paint on the canvas. Van Gogh used the strokes of his brush or palette knife to try to portray emotions in the paint itself.

exhibitions that he left Paris and went back to his home town of Aix-en-Provence. Although he agreed with the Impressionists about painting from nature, he was not happy with their style. He wanted to find a way to return to the balanced design of the earlier masters. He did not like the hazy outlines of Impressionist paintings, yet he did not want to go back to the traditional styles of drawing. He also wanted to capture the rich, sunbaked colors of Southern France. He experimented with different ideas until he succeeded in achieving structure, balance and depth in his paintings, as well as using bright colors.

Another painter who studied the work of the Impressionists was a Dutch man called Vincent van Gogh (1853-90). Excited by the idea of painting the bright sunny colors of southern France, he went to the town of Arles. He painted feverishly, using color to portray his emotions. But excited though he was by his work, he was lonely and had fits of madness and depression.

ART IN THE TWENTIETH CENTURY

ART EVENTS	WORLD EVENTS
1900 20TH CENTURY	
	World Exhibition in Paris
	First flight of Zeppelin airship (1900)
Picasso's first Paris exhibition (1901)	Marconi sends first wireless message across Atlantic (1901)
Exhibition by *Les Fauves* (the wild beasts) Paris (1905)	
Picasso's first Cubist painting shocks art world (1907).	*Titanic* sinks on first voyage. (1912)
Dadaist Movement begins as result of war.	World War I (1914-18)
Surrealist Movement introduced by Dali and others (1924).	Vladimir K. Zworykin demonstrated the first practical television system (1929).
	Frank Whittle patents jet engine (1930).
Many European artists leave for the United States.	World War II (1939-45)
New York becomes center of art world.	
Jackson Pollock develops his abstract style "action painting." (1947)	Independent India was founded (1947).
Warhol and others introduce Pop Art (early 1960s).	President Kennedy assassinated. (1963)
Tate Gallery, London, displays 120 fire bricks laid in an oblong (1976).	First supersonic flight by the Concorde across the Atlantic (1976)
Manet painting sells for £7.5 million (over $10 million) in London.	
Artists such as Lucian Freud return to "unflinching realism" in painting.	Berlin Wall comes down (1989).

THE WILD BEASTS

Paris was the center of the art world at the beginning of the 20th century. In 1905 a group of artists held an exhibition there that was to herald the beginning of a new movement. This group came to be known as *Les Fauves* (the wild beasts) after an art critic at the 1905 exhibition saw a sculpture by Donatello (see page 67) surrounded by brilliantly colored paintings and remarked that it looked like "Donatello among the wild beasts." The Fauves artists liked violent colors and designs. The most famous of these painters was Henri Matisse (1869-1954). Matisse painted subjects such as interiors, stilllifes and people, but he changed what he saw into patterns, using strong, vibrant colors.

Matisse's use of color shocked many people at the time he was working. He used large areas of plain, bright colors which often bore little resemblance to the colors of things in real life. For example,

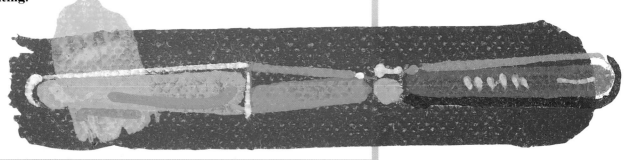

THE SCREAM

The Norwegian artist Edvard Munch (1863-1944), painted a famous picture called *The Scream*. It shows a terrified face which looks almost like a skull. The lines all around the screaming person give the impression that the scenery is screaming, too. The picture has the feeling of a nightmare. People were upset by this kind of art because it was not beautiful and it made them face up to ugly and violent emotions.

Red Interior by Henri Matisse. Matisse used color in his paintings in a completely new way, not to imitate what he saw, but to convey how he felt.

a portrait of Madame Matisse showed her with a vivid green stripe running down her forehead and nose. However, Matisse was using color in a new way, not to imitate what he saw around him, but to express what he felt. This new use of color influenced many later 20th-century artists.

TOWARD ABSTRACT ART

The next big question asked by artists was whether a picture needed a subject at all. Could an idea be created by using colors and shapes alone? One of the first artists to try out this idea was the Russian painter Wassily Kandinsky (1866-1944). He thought that a painting made up purely of colors and shapes was like a piece of music, with different meanings for different people. His paintings do not represent anything recognizable. Instead, they speak directly to the observer's mind. This was the beginning of "abstract" art.

PABLO PICASSO

Pablo Picasso (1881-1973) was born in Spain. He showed himself to be a talented artist as a child, and when he was 19 years old, he went to Paris to paint. He experimented with different styles, for a time painting melancholy subjects such as starving beggars and sick children in shades of blue (known as his "Blue Period"). During a happier time, he used reds and pinks (his "Pink Period") to paint more cheerful subjects such as dancers and circus performers. It did not take Picasso long to become successful, but he was constantly looking for new inspiration. He became interested in African masks, that were being shown in Europe for the first time, particularly in the simple but expressive way that they distorted the human face.

NEW IDEAS

Picasso saw that it was possible to build up a different type of image using simple lines and angular shapes. In 1907, he shocked the world with his painting *Les Demoiselles d'Avignon*. *Les Demoiselles* is a

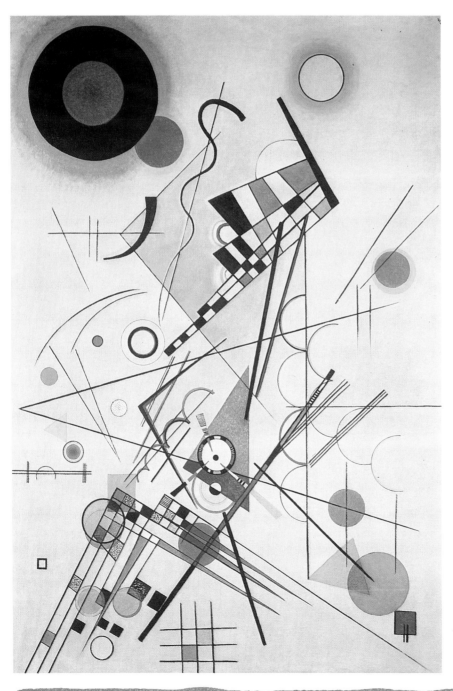

Composition 8 *by Wassily Kandinsky. Kandinsky was one of the first artists to experiment with purely abstract art.*

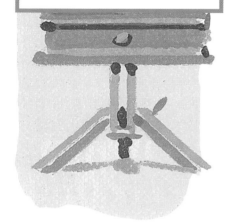

painting of five women. There was nothing new about that—but the way they were painted certainly was new. No one had seen anything like it before. This painting marked the beginning of a new movement that became known as Cubism after an art critic who saw one of Picasso's paintings said that the surface of the painting was divided up into "little cubes."

In his painting, Picasso breaks the bodies of the five women into angular shapes. He paints different parts of the bodies from different angles—for example, the eyes are all painted from the front even if the figure is facing sideways. The noses are all in profile. Two of the women wear masks like the African masks that inspired Picasso's work. Even though this picture is not realistic, we understand what it is meant to be. Unlike Kandinsky, who wanted to use color and shape in a completely "abstract" way, Picasso uses a recognizable subject and then interprets it in a completely new way.

CUBISM DEVELOPS

Picasso continued to experiment with Cubism. He often worked with another painter, Georges Braque (1882-1963), producing paintings in colors such as blacks, browns, and grays. The French artist Robert Delaunay (1885-1941), who was a friend of Picasso and Braque, experimented with brighter colors. Delaunay was interested in mechanical things, and one of his favorite subjects was the Eiffel Tower in Paris. The Eiffel Tower was still quite new when Delaunay painted it (it was built in 1889). He used reds and oranges and yellows and painted it from many different angles at once. It looks hectic and chaotic, as though the tower might fall down at any moment. The effect is dramatic and exciting.

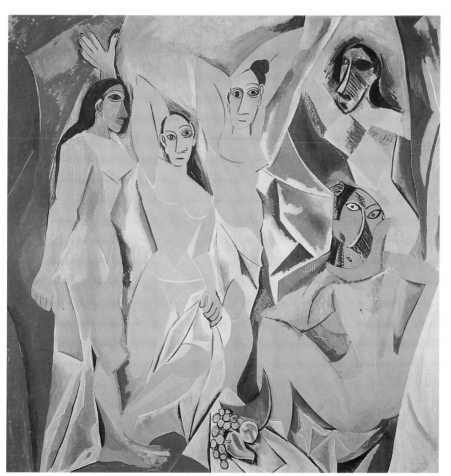

Les Demoiselles d'Avignon *by Pablo Picasso. Picasso breaks up the bodies of the women into angular shapes.*

CONNECTIONS

A development from Cubism was collage, in which artists combined painting and drawing with other materials such as scraps of cloth and newsprint. Matisse (see page 44) also experimented with collage, cutting and tearing shapes from large pieces of colored paper.

GEORGIA O'KEEFFE

Georgia O'Keeffe (1887-1986) was an American artist who began painting in New York during the 1920s. She is known best for her huge close-up images of single flower heads. She took her inspiration from the world around her—skyscrapers in New York, country landscapes—then simplified the forms and shapes so that the outcome was more of an abstract image.

ANTI-ART

During World War I (1914-18) many artists tried to express their feelings about the horror of war and the waste of life. They wanted to attack a society that could let this happen. The first groups were started in Zurich, Switzerland, by the poet Tristan Tzara and the painter and sculptor Jean Hans Arp (1887-1966) and in New York by painter Marcel Duchamp

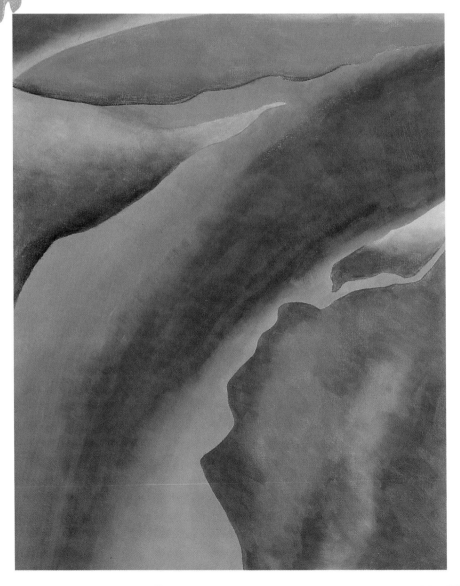

Only One by Georgia O'Keeffe. O'Keeffe simplified forms and shapes to produce an abstract image.

The Human Condition *by René Magritte*

The Disintegration of the Persistence of Memory *by Salvador Dali*

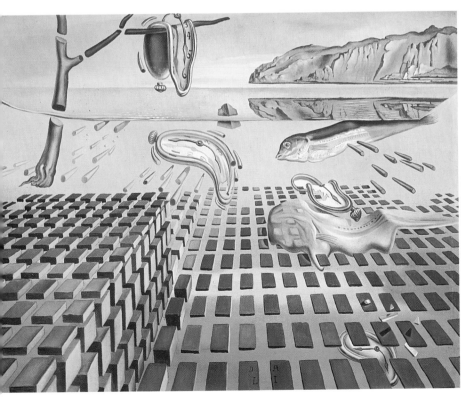

(1887-1968). Dadaism set out to shock and mock the pretentiousness of the established art world. Arp tore up pieces of paper and let them fall to the floor to create a "work of art." Duchamp exhibited everyday objects, such as a snow shovel, with a title and his signature. They also used junk in their work, sometimes to make collages (see box).

AN ECCENTRIC GENIUS

Another movement was founded in Paris in 1924 by a group of artists who painted dreamlike pictures in which people and objects merge together in a fantastic way. This movement became known as Surrealism. A leading Surrealist artist was the Spaniard, Salvador Dali (1904-89). Dali was an eccentric who painted pictures with a nightmarish quality to them. Before he went to art school in the 1920s, he wrote in his diary, "I'll be a genius . . . Perhaps I'll be despised and misunderstood, but I'll be a genius, a great genius." Many people found his work hard to understand yet they were fascinated by it. Other Surrealists were the Belgian artist, René Magritte (1898-1967), and the Spaniard, Joan Miró (1893-1983).

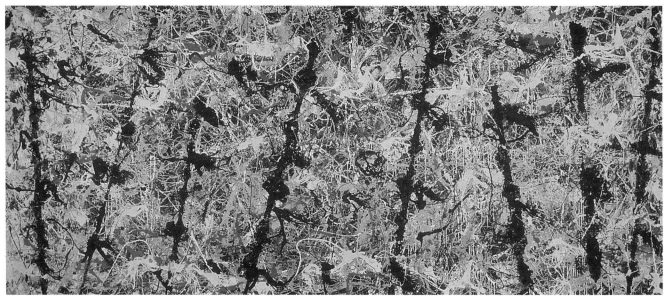

Blue Poles, 1952 *by Jackson Pollock*

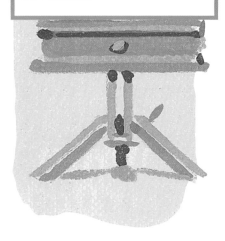

TWISTING LINES

With the outbreak of World War II in 1939, many artists left Europe for the United States, and New York became an artistic center. These artists brought with them views based on Cubism, Surrealism, and abstract art. These ideas inspired the American painter, Jackson Pollock (1912-56). Pollock had been interested in Surrealism but he gradually turned to more abstract work. He created many of his pictures by putting the canvas on the floor and dripping, pouring, or throwing paint onto it. The result was a jumble of twisting lines and colors. Jackson Pollock was killed in a car crash in 1956. His wife, the painter Lee Krasner (1908-84), also experimented with abstract painting. She covered her canvases in hectic, lively marks, but her work was not widely recognized during Pollock's lifetime.

Mark Rothko (1903-70) was a Russian painter who emigrated to the United States in 1913. His paintings are very different from Jackson Pollock's. They are made up of oblongs of color, which convey a mood, rather than the energy seen in Pollock's pictures. Rothko said that he was interested only "in expressing basic human emotions, tragedy, ecstasy, doom, and so on. . . ." Shortly before his death, Rothko completed a group of murals for the intedenominational Rothko Chapel in Houston, Texas.

Another American, Helen Frankenthaler (1928-), was influenced by Jackson Pollock and Arshile Gorky (see Glossary of artists) but developed her own style. She introduced a technique of staining untreated canvas with thin paint, so that it seeped in rather than staying on the surface. She also used transparent stains so that parts of the canvas showed through. The effect is of floating color.

Whaam! by Roy Lichtenstein. In his paintings, Lichtenstein enlarges the kind of images more usually found in comic strips.

POP ART

In the early 1960s some artists turned away from abstract art and instead concentrated on everyday objects. This became known as Pop Art. The most famous of all the Pop artists were the Americans, Andy Warhol (*c.* 1928-87) and Roy Lichtenstein (1923-). Warhol often painted subjects from advertising and the media, such as soup cans and repeated images of Marilyn Monroe and Elvis Presley. Lichtenstein took his inspiration from the images used in comics. The British artist David Hockney (1937-) has also become internationally famous for his paintings of the world he lives in.

ART IN THE 1980s

During the 1980s, artists began to look again at the trends of the 20th century. Early in the century, artists were out to shock the established art world. However, by the 1970s these trends had become an acceptable part of "modern art." Some people still found styles such as Abstract Expressionism difficult to understand, but they were no longer shocked by the departure from conventional art. Some artists returned to a more traditional approach to painting by moving away from abstract images to more recognizable images, often of figures.

Many artists continued to portray the harshness of life—loneliness, desolation, and fear—as well as the brighter side.

Marilyn by Andy Warhol, one of a series of silk screen prints made of the famous actress, Marilyn Monroe.

CONNECTIONS

Op art is short for "optical" art because it is concerned with the way we see things, and the "tricks" that some images play on our eyes. Of course, the effects of optical illusion have been used for centuries to create depth in pictures (see page 17). But op artists such as Bridget Riley (1931-) use patterns, lines, and color to create unsettling illusions of movement and distortion which can have a quite hypnotic effect!

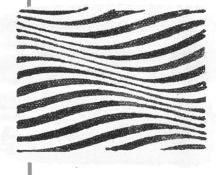

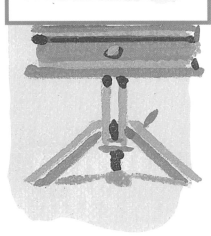

Self-portrait by Francis Bacon. Bacon massively distorts the features of his own face to create an alarming gargoyle.

Lucian Freud (1922-) has painted portraits, stilllifes, and landscapes, but his most powerful paintings are of real men and women, with all their physical flaws, but always looking as though they could step out of the picture. Lucian Freud has a particular talent for showing color tones, particularly of human skin.

Francis Bacon (1909-92) was a quite different kind of painter. In his pictures he portrayed despair and violence, and his subjects were sometimes hideous and disturbing to look at. He developed a technique of smudging the paint on the canvas with a rag, and applying the paint in thick and thin layers on the same canvas to give a dramatic contrast.

You can find out about art in the 1990s in the last chapter (pages 80-3).

CRAFTS

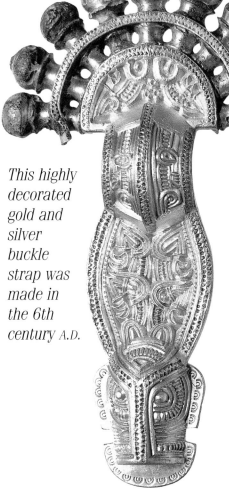

This highly decorated gold and silver buckle strap was made in the 6th century A.D.

Craft working goes back to the beginning of civilization. People began to farm the land about 12,000 years ago (see page 18). The first farmers needed tools, pots, and baskets for storing food, clothes, and shoes. And so craft workers began to produce these objects to exchange for food. As towns and cities grew up and people became more wealthy, they showed their status by wearing beautiful jewelry or carrying decorated weapons. Many towns and cities had an area where all the craftworkers lived and worked.

Craft workers worked with natural materials. They learned to make leather from animal skins and to weave grasses and reeds into baskets. They learned how to shape clay into pots and dishes, and later they learned to make glass. They learned how to spin and weave fibers into cloth and how to dye the cloth with bright vegetable dyes. They learned how to work metal and to carve wood. Today many craftworkers continue traditions that have been practiced for centuries.

POTTERY

Pottery is one of the oldest crafts. Thousands of years ago, people realized that they could shape clay into pots and bake them in the sun or in a bonfire to harden the clay. Once the clay has been baked, it will never soften again.

The earliest types of pots were pinch pots. The potter rolled some clay into a small ball and then hollowed out the center with a thumb. These pots could hold small amounts of food or liquid, but people soon began to experiment with coil pots for storing grain and other foods. To make a coil pot, the potter rolled out sausage-shaped strips of clay and coiled them, one above the other, around a circular base. When the pot was finished, the potter smoothed over the connections between the coils.

A skilful potter shapes a pot on a modern wheel.

THE POTTER'S WHEEL

The potter's wheel was invented in Mesopotamia in about 3500 B.C. The wheel was a round, flat stone on a shaft, which was fixed to the ground. Modern potter's wheels are powered by electricity, but the earliest wheels had to be turned by hand. Pots could be made much faster on a wheel than they could by coiling, and they could also be formed into a bigger variety of shapes.

CONNECTIONS

Many people distinguish between crafts and "fine art." Crafts are usually described as decorative objects with a practical, everyday use. "Fine art" is painting, sculpture, or music.

FIRING THE CLAY

Baking pottery in the sun or in an open fire had one disadvantage. The pots were not baked, or fired, at a high enough temperature to make them water-resistant. This meant that they could be used only for storing dry goods, such as grain. The baked clay was still porous, like a sponge, so liquids soaked into it. To make a pot water-resistant, it needed to be fired at a far higher temperature. The answer was a closed oven called a kiln. The kiln was probably invented in China in about 4500 B.C. It had two chambers, an upper chamber to hold the pots and the lower one where the fire burned.

GLAZES

A glaze makes pottery completely watertight. The first glazes were used in Egypt about 2,000 years ago. Glaze is a kind of liquid glass, which is painted onto the pot and forms a hard, shiny, protective surface when it is fired. Some glazes are transparent and highlight the color of the clay. Others look transparent when they are painted on but change color when they are fired. The color of the glaze depends on what it is made from, the kind of clay being used to make the pot, and the heat of the kiln.

NOT JUST POTS

Craft workers became extremely skilled at working with clay and with techniques of firing and glazing.

A pottery jar from China, made during the T'ang Dynasty (A.D. 618-906).

CONNECTIONS

In the Islamic faith it is forbidden to portray the prophet Muhammad, or to have any portraits in holy places. As a result, Muslim artists developed a great skill in using geometric patterns, combined with the beautiful flowing shapes of Arabic script, usually taken from the Muslim holy book, the *Koran*.

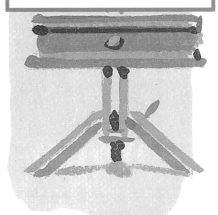

As the centuries passed, the art of the potter was not confined to making pots. All over the world we can find examples of different uses for clay. These range from the practical—7000 years ago in Mesopotamia, people made sickles from clay—to the ornamental. In Africa the Nok people made sculptures of heads out of a kind of clay called terra cotta. In South America the people of the Moche culture made portrait pots in the shape of human figures, with details added in paint. In China, figures and objects made from clay were placed in the tombs of wealthy people. These models included houses, camels, horses, musicians, acrobats, jugglers, and merchants.

In Islamic countries such as Iran and Turkey, clay tiles were used to cover the walls and ceilings of mosques and palaces. The tiles were glazed in brilliant

A terra-cotta head made by the Nok people of Nigeria

THE TERRA-COTTA ARMY

One of the most spectacular finds in recent years was a whole army made from a type of pottery called terra cotta. The army was uncovered in 1974 in China. The terra cotta army was made to guard the tomb of the first emperor of China, Shi Huang Di, who ruled from 221 to 206 B.C. About 700,000 workers built Shi Huang Di's underground tomb and sculptors made more than 8,000 life-sized soldiers, some with horses.

Part of Shi Huang Di's terra-cotta army

A panel of 24 tiles from Isnik in Turkey

colors and often arranged to form geometric patterns. Sometimes the tiles were cut up and used to make a kind of mosaic. In other places whole tiles were colored and patterned to form one huge design.

PORCELAIN

Porcelain is a fine, white, delicate type of pottery. It is often called "china" because it was first made in China in about A.D. 900. Porcelain is made from a white clay, called kaolin. It is fired at a very high temperature so that the kaolin becomes hard and glasslike.

Huge amounts of Chinese porcelain were exported to Europe in the 16th, 17th, and 18th centuries. European potters tried to imitate the fine china, but the method of making porcelain remained a puzzle until a German chemist, Johann Böttger, discovered the secret in 1708. The first European porcelain factory was opened at Meissen in Germany. Reserves of the white clay, kaolin, were found in Limoges, France, in 1752 and a few years later in Cornwall, England. Porcelain is still made in these centers.

This porcelain dish was made in China in the 18th century for export to Europe. It shows a whale hunt.

GLASS

Glass is made from a mixture of silica (sand), soda ash, and crushed limestone. When the silica is heated to a very high temperature, it melts into liquid glass, which can be molded into shape. The glass hardens as it cools. Soda ash is added to strengthen the glass. Silica will only melt at a temperature of 1500°C, so limestone is added to lower the melting point and harden the glass.

Glass was first made in Mesopotamia about 2600 B.C. but it was the Egyptians who first learned how to shape glass in clay casts and to make patterned glass in different colors.

CONNECTIONS

There were glassmakers in Venice, Italy, from the 10th century, and it became a famous center for glass in the 15th century (see page 29). Venetian glass was very fine but extremely workable. This allowed Venetian glassmakers to create exquisite, intricate objects in glass.

GLASS BLOWING

Glass blowing was invented in about 100 B.C., probably in Syria. This technique is still used today to make objects such as glasses and vases. A blob of molten glass is put on the end of a hollow tube called a blowing iron. The glass blower blows down the tube, and the air inflates the blob of glass, like blowing up a balloon. The glass bubble is pulled into shape while it is still on the blowing iron.

The Romans were skilled glassmakers. They perfected the art of glass blowing, often blowing the glass into a mold to make elaborately shaped vessels. One of the best-known examples of Roman glass is the Portland Vase. This is an example of cameo glass. A layer of blue glass was blown and covered with a thin layer of white glass. The white glass was then carved away to create the mythical scenes that cover the vase.

The Portland Vase. It was probably made between 27 B.C. and A.D. 37 in Alexandria, which was an important center of ancient glass making. In 1845 the vase was smashed into over 200 bits, but was carefully restored to its former glory.

A mask from Papua New Guinea. It is made from tortoise-shell held together with strips of palm.

Masks

Masks have been made for thousands of years. Some were worn by people taking part in religious rituals. Others were used by actors in the theater, for example in Ancient Greece. Today masks are still used widely—for example in rituals in many parts of the world, in the Japanese Noh theater, or in masked dances. Masks can be made from any material— wood, papier-maché, basketwork, cloth, leather, and they usually cover the face or head of the wearer. Often a mask is part of an elaborate costume. Some masks are huge—for example, the masks that hang on houses in Papua New Guinea to frighten away evil spirits. Others are tiny; during dance rituals Inuit women in northern Alaska often wore small finger masks on their hands. In ritual ceremonies the person wearing a particular mask is believed to become the spirit or animal or idea represented by the mask. In many traditional societies only the men are permitted to wear masks.

Japanese actors often wear masks in Noh and similar kinds of theatre.

Bundles of brightly colored silk for sale at a market in China

Unraveling silk cocoons in a factory in Xinjiang, China

TEXTILES

The first textiles were made from natural fibers such as flax, cotton, wool, and silk. They were spun by hand and woven into cloth on a loom. Today most of the textiles we buy are made in factories, but craft-workers all over the world continue to use age-old methods of making and decorating textiles.

The flax plant is used to make linen. Cotton comes from the cotton plant, which has seed heads containing fluffy balls of cotton fiber. The fibers have to be cleaned and then straightened using a method called carding. They are then twisted together on a spindle to form a continuous length of yarn. Wool is spun in the same way. Silk fiber is produced by the silkworm when it spins its cocoon. The cocoon is made of a single strand of silk, which is about 985 feet long. The thread, called the filament, is unraveled, and several filaments are twisted together to make a yarn strong enough to be woven into cloth.

All these natural fibers have been used for thousands of years. Cotton was originally grown in India and in Central America. The Ancient Egyptians made cloth from flax and from imported cotton. In many parts of the world, wool is obtained from sheep, but in South America people continue to make fine, warm woolen cloth from the fleeces of alpaca, vicuña, and llama.

WEAVING

Weaving involves passing horizontal threads (the weft) over and under vertical threads (the warp). The warp threads are put on to a frame called a loom to keep them tight and straight. For a plain weave, a stick is passed under every other warp thread to hold the threads apart so that the weft can be passed through more quickly. Patterns are created by varying the pattern of the warp threads or by using different colored threads.

Silkworms are native to China, and for thousands of years the method of silk production was kept secret. Silk cloth was highly prized by the Ancient Greeks and Romans, but it wasn't until around the 7th century A.D. that the secret of silk production spread to the West.

DYEING YARN AND TEXTILES

There are two ways of putting color into textiles. One is to dye the yarn before it is woven, and the other is to dye the woven fabric. Before the 19th century, when chemical dyes were introduced, all cloth was colored with natural dyes from plants. Natural dyes are made by squeezing the liquid out of berries and other parts of plants. Dye does not take to fabric very well on its own, and so it is mixed with a substance called a mordant. Salt and vinegar can both be used as mordants.

Drawing on a design with a t'junting to make batik cloth

There are many traditional ways of making patterns on fabric. Batik is an ancient Indonesian craft. Areas of the fabric are covered with hot wax to protect them from the dye. Designs are drawn into the melted wax with a hollow tool called a t'junting and a brush. When the wax has hardened, the fabric is dipped into dye. The process can be repeated time after time to produce different colored patterns on the fabric. The wax is then removed and the fabric is laid out to dry.

A traditional batik design from central Java, Indonesia

Making tie-dye fabric in India. You can see some examples of beautiful tie-dye fabrics in the background.

Tie-dye is another method of producing colored patterns on fabric. Parts of the fabric are rolled up tightly and tied so that the dye cannot reach them. Ikat is an ancient craft which originated in central Asia over 3,000 years ago. The patterns on ikat cloth are made by dyeing the threads before they are woven. The threads are bundled and tied so that the dye

DYES

Most natural dyes are made from plants:

Madder: red. Made from the roots of the madder plant.

Woad: blue. Made from the leaves of the woad plant.

Indigo: blue. Made from the leaves of the indigo shrub. Indigo doesn't need a mordant (see main text) to fix the color to the cloth. Huge amounts of indigo were imported to Europe from India.

Orchil/litmus: red and blue/purple. Made from lichens, these dyes change color according to their treatment.

Fustic: yellow. Made from a plant imported to Europe from Central America.

Tyrian purple: Not made from a plant but from a small snail that once lived on the shores of the eastern Mediterranean. Tyrian purple was so highly prized by the Romans that only the highest-ranking officials were permitted to wear it.

A jacket made from ikat cloth

doesn't touch some areas. When the threads are woven, the cloth has bands of pattern and color.

CONNECTIONS

William Morris (1834-96) was a British designer and artist, who started a firm of decorators and designers in 1861. He preferred to make things by hand rather than using the new industrial methods that had taken over in Great Britain (see page 38). He designed stained glass, carpets, and furniture and patterns for fabrics and wallpaper, which are still used today. His work inspired the Arts and Crafts Movement in England, which revived medieval methods of craftworking.

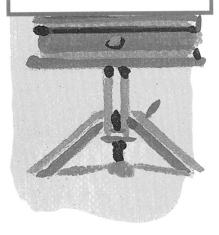

PRINTING ON FABRIC

Fabric can also be decorated by printing patterns on it. One method is silk-screen printing. A design is cut out of paper and laid onto the fabric. A piece of silk stretched across a screen is put on top of the fabric and paint is forced through the silk. The paint colors only the parts not covered by the paper design. A new screen is used for each color in the pattern.

Block printing is a way of producing intricate, repetitive patterns on fabric. It has been used in India for centuries. A raised design is carved on to a block of wood and the wood is dipped in ink. The printer presses the wood onto the fabric. More ink is put on the block and it is pressed on to another part of the fabric.

METALWORK

It is thought that metals were first worked in western Asia over 10,000 years ago. People found small lumps of copper in the ground, and learned to shape them to make tools or ornaments. Around 3500 B.C. a new method of working metal was developed. This may have happened because potters, in their search for new materials, put lumps of gold or copper into their kilns (see page 54). They found that the metal melted when it was heated and hardened when it cooled. Then they discovered that metal could be taken out of rock ore by the same process. This is known as smelting.

A vessel made from bronze by Chinese metalworkers of the Shang Dynasty (1650-1027 B.C.)

WOODWORKING

Wood has been carved into practical and ornamental objects since prehistoric times. Early woodworkers used simple stone knives and axes. People gradually invented better tools with which they could carve intricate designs. They also learned how to make larger articles such as chairs and tables.

By about 3000 B.C., metalworkers in Asia had discovered how to make bronze by mixing copper with tin to form an alloy, which was stronger than copper alone. Metalworkers in China perfected the art of making highly decorated bronze vessels in molds. First they made a clay model of the vessel itself, and then they made clay molds in sections. The clay molds were pieced together, and then the molten metal was poured in and left to harden.

Iron can only be melted at very high temperatures, and we do not know exactly when people began to smelt iron. We do know, however, that iron was being used to make tools and ornaments in central Europe by around 1400 B.C. Iron tools were stronger than tools made from the softer metals in bronze.

Metalworkers of Benin

In western Africa the kingdom of Benin (in present-day Nigeria) was at the height of its power in the 14th through 17th centuries. The king, or *oba*, lived in a palace sumptuously decorated with plaques and sculptures made from bronze. These bronze artifacts were made by skilled craft workers by the "lost wax" process. This involved making a perfect wax model of the object, then surrounding the wax with clay. When the clay hardened, the wax was melted out of the middle. Then molten metal was poured into the clay mold. This process allowed craft workers to make intricate patterns and designs in the soft wax, which were then reproduced in the hard metal. Some of the finest Benin bronzes are made from metal no thicker than thin paper.

One of the bronze plaques made to decorate the palace of the king of Benin in Africa

SCULPTURE

Sculpture is the art of shaping or modeling using materials such as stone, wood, clay, or metal. Sculptures can be in relief, which means that the figures or objects are carved out of a background of stone, metal, or wood, or they can be free-standing. In this chapter we look mainly at stone sculpture. You can find out more about the use of clay, metal, and wood in the "Crafts" chapter (pages 53-63).

TOOLS AND METHODS

To carve a hard material such as stone requires a variety of tools. First, the sculptor cuts out the rough shape of the sculpture with axes and cutting hammers. To put in the detail, the sculptor uses chisels and hammers. Soft stone has to be treated delicately so that it does not crumble into pieces. The sculptor uses a wooden hammer called a maul to tap the chisel.

Sometimes a sculpture is cast in metal. First, the sculpture is modeled in wax or clay. If wax is used, the model is covered in a mold of clay or plaster. This mold is fired to a high temperature, and the wax melts out. The hot metal can then be poured in its place. A similar method is used for clay models.

Relief carvings decorate a staircase in the ruins of Persepolis, in modern-day Iran.

The huge, ancient sculptures at Abu Simbel, Egypt

ANCIENT SCULPTURES

The earliest sculptures are between 27,000 and 30,000 years old. They are small carved figures of people and animals that were probably used for religious rituals. There are also examples of sculpture from many ancient civilizations. For example, the ruins of the ancient city of Persepolis, in modern-day Iran, are covered in relief sculptures showing the lavish ceremonies held in the palace at the center of the city. The Ancient Egyptians decorated their temples and tombs with larger-than-life statues of their pharaohs, such as the massive figures of Ramses II at Abu Simbel.

CONNECTIONS

Although most Greek sculpture has come down to us as clear white marble, there is evidence that it was actually highly painted in bright colors.

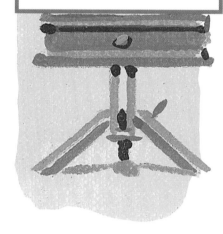

CLASSICAL GREECE

Some of the finest statues known today were sculpted in Ancient Greece after about 500 B.C. (see page 20). Greek sculptors studied the human body and the way the muscles work to make their statues accurate and lifelike. A statue of a discus thrower, the *Discobolos*, illustrates this point very well. This statue was carved by the sculptor Myron in about 450 B.C. The athlete's body is twisted around as his arm goes back with the discus. You can see the power in the muscles of his arm and upper body as he prepares to throw it. However, the expression on his face is serene and emotionless.

Even though much Greek art was destroyed when Greece was conquered by the Romans, many pieces were copied by Roman sculptors. This work served as an inspiration to later artists, particularly during the Renaissance in Italy (see page 21).

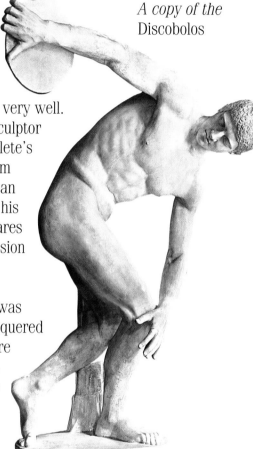

A copy of the Discobolos

THE PARTHENON

In the 400s B.C., a statesman called Pericles was the leader of the city-state of Athens (the modern capital of Greece). He commissioned the sculptor Phidias to oversee the carving of marble statues for his new temple, the Parthenon. Among the 500 statues sculpted for the new temple was a 40-foot high statue of Athena, the goddess to whom the temple was dedicated. Phidias also carved scenes from Athenian life to decorate the top of the temple.

66 THE WORLD OF ART

CONNECTIONS

The man who became known as Buddha was a rich, young Indian prince called Siddhartha Gautama (c. 563-c. 483 B.C.). When he was 29, he turned his back on wealth and luxury to find enlightenment. Followers of the Buddha spread his teachings throughout India and beyond. Today Buddhism is a major world religion with over 400 million believers.

INDIAN SCULPTURE

There are examples of Indian sculpture that are over 4,000 years old, from the earliest civilization in the region, in the Indus Valley. The Hindu religion became established in India between 1000 and 500 B.C. Throughout India there are elaborate Hindu temples covered with exquisite statues and relief decorations, all of which have a meaning or a story to tell. In some places these temples are carved out of soapstone. This stone is soft and workable when it is taken out of the ground, allowing the sculptor to carve very fine details, but it gradually hardens and darkens in the air.

Buddhism also inspired religious sculpture in India. However, at first artists were not permitted to portray the Buddha himself. Instead, sculptors carved symbols to represent the Buddha and scenes from his life. In the 2nd century A.D., artists in northwestern India became influenced by the sculpture of the Greeks. At this time sculptors began to carve images of the Buddha (see page 8), often draped in beautiful, flowing robes.

The tradition of stonecarving is very strong in India, and images of the gods are still made according to the ancient rules. There are communities of craft workers who specialize in making statues and fine sculpture for temples. In some areas elaborate stonework is also used to decorate palaces and houses.

Intricate carvings cover the outside of a temple in India.

CHRISTIAN SCULPTURE

During the 11th century work began on some of the great cathedrals of Europe (see page 25). Romanesque churches were decorated with magnificent sculptures designed to teach people about the Christian religion. During the 12th century increased wealth from trade led to the growth of towns, the founding of universities, and the building of even finer cathedrals in the Gothic style, such as Chartres in northern France.

It took so long to build a huge cathedral such as Chartres that you can see by walking around the building how styles of sculpture changed over the years! The west front of Chartres Cathedral was the first part of the cathedral to be built and decorated, in the 1140s and 1150s. The statues of saints that surround the doorways are very narrow and upright, like columns. Each one was carved out of a single block of stone, and each one has the same fine, pleated drapery and same facial expression. Eighty years later, sculptors were busy carving statues for the north and south sides of the cathedral. Each of these statues has a different expression, different clothing, and some are even turned toward each other, as if in conversation!

Statues from the west front of Chartres Cathedral in France (above). Compare these statues to those carved slightly later for the north porch (right).

THE RENAISSANCE

Roman sculptures in Italian cities inspired artists to look back to Classical styles, sparking off the period now known as the Renaissance. The finest sculptor of the group of artists based in Florence was Donatello (*c.* 1386-1466). Donatello went to Rome with Brunelleschi (see page 28) to study Classical art. When he returned to Florence, he was commissioned by Cosimo de' Medici to make a bronze

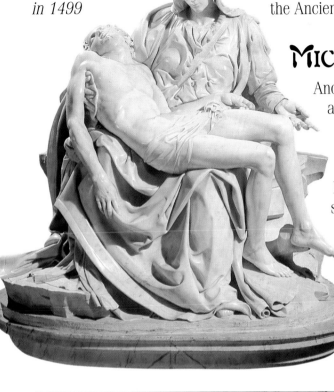

The Pietà, *sculpted by Michelangelo in 1499*

statue, called the *David*. This is thought to be the first nude, free-standing statue that had been sculpted since the time of the Ancient Romans.

MICHELANGELO

Another important Renaissance artist was the painter and sculptor Michelangelo Buonarroti (see page 29). As a boy, Michelangelo was trained in Florence at the workshop of the painter Domenico Ghirlandaio (1449-94), a leading master of the earlier Renaissance. But Michelangelo's real love was sculpture. He studied the human body in great detail, and by the time he was in his twenties, he was already famous for sculptures such as the *Pietà* in St. Peter's, Rome. Michelangelo worked in a smooth, white marble, which was quarried at Carrara in central Italy. He often went to Carrara to choose the marble for a particular statue. Michelangelo had a strong sense that the statues were already inside the great blocks of marble, just waiting for him to chip away the stone around them. He had a particular method of carving marble by removing the stone from one viewpoint only, rather like seeing an object in a bath of water with the water slowly draining away to reveal the finished object appearing out of one surface.

SCULPTING THE SUN

Gianlorenzo Bernini (1598-1680) was one of the most influential artists of the 17th century. He was not only a sculptor but also an architect, painter, playwright, and designer of fireworks displays! Unlike the Renaissance sculptors who carved each sculpture from one block of stone, Bernini often used several pieces of stone to create his giant sculptures. This gave him much greater freedom to carve expansive gestures, such as figures with wide, outspread arms.

Bernini designed and carved the main altarpiece, the Pope's chair, St. Peter's Colonnde, and many tombs for St. Peter's in Rome. He often included carvings of the sun's rays in his sculptures, as a dramatic backdrop to the main figures.

Bernini's The Vision of St Theresa *which rises above one of the altars in a small church in Rome*

ANTONIO CANOVA

In the late 18th century, there was a reaction to what many artists saw as the frivolity of Baroque and Rococo art, and once again artists looked back to the Ancient Romans and Greeks for their inspiration. Antonio Canova (1757-1822) was one of the sculptors who worked in the Neoclassical style. He worked in marble that was polished with pumice stone to make it shine. Canova sculpted Napoleon Bonaparte in the style of a Roman emperor, and Napoleon's sister, Pauline Bonaparte Borghese, as the goddess Venus.

CONNECTIONS

At the beginning of the 19th century, a British diplomat called Thomas Bruce, Earl of Elgin, made a remarkable purchase. He bought many of the ancient sculptures made for the Parthenon in Athens, Greece (see page 65). At the time, Greece was under Turkish rule, and Bruce feared that the statues would be damaged or destroyed if they were not removed. The British Museum eventually bought the sculptures, now known as the Elgin Marbles. Today there is a campaign for the marbles to be returned to Greece.

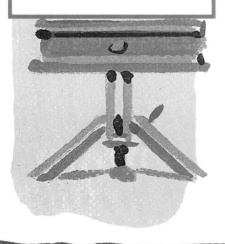

AUGUSTE RODIN

The French sculptor Auguste Rodin (1840-1917) was one of the greatest sculptors of his time. He was born in the same year as the painter Claude Monet (see page 41), and his work was often criticized in the same breath as the works of the Impressionists.

Rodin was inspired by Michelangelo's work and created his sculptures in a similar way, releasing them from the stone prison in which he believed they were held. Some of Rodin's works look as though the statue has only half emerged from the stone. Rodin was interested in expressing inner feelings through his sculptures, even if this meant distorting some of the features of his subjects. However, he was also capable of sculpting figures with perfect forms, such as in his famous sculpture *The Kiss*.

The Thinker *by Auguste Rodin*

EXPERIMENTS WITH SCULPTURE

During the late 19th and 20th centuries, sculptors began to experiment with new ideas, just as painters did. Constantin Brancusi (1876-1957) was a Romanian sculptor, who worked in Paris for most of his life. His sculptures are very simple and streamlined, making use of the original shape and the quality of the material, be it stone, wood, or metal. Brancusi inspired many other 20th-century sculptors to experiment with "abstract" forms in sculpture.

The American sculptor, Alexander Calder (1898-1976) made mobile sculptures. Calder's mobiles were delicately balanced and weighted so that they moved in the air. Through this movement, Calder wanted to show that the universe is always moving but is held together by balancing forces. Examples of Calder's mobiles hang outside and in buildings all over the world.

The Kiss by Constantin Brancusi. Can you see the two lovers embracing?

Sculptures by Alexander Calder, including a mobile sculpture (right) called Little Janey-Waney

HENRY MOORE

One of the greatest 20th-century artists was the British sculptor Henry Moore (1898-1986). Moore took his inspiration from many sources including Brancusi, ancient American sculpture, and, most of all, the natural world and the human figure. Many

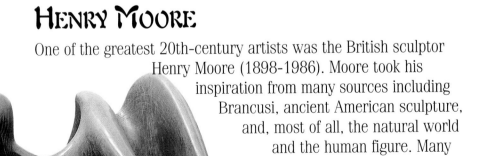

Reclining Figure, a sculpture in bronze by Henry Moore

Involute 1 *by Barbara Hepworth*

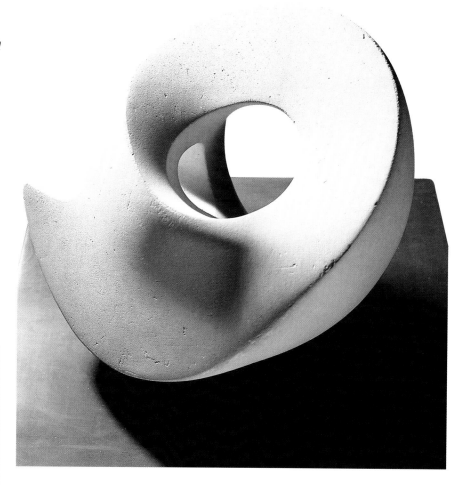

CONNECTIONS

The British sculptor, Anthony Caro (1924-) worked with Henry Moore and then spent some time traveling around the United States where he met artists such as Helen Frankenthaler (see page 50). He originally worked in clay, but as his sculptures became more and more abstract, he decided to experiment with a new material— steel. Since the 1960s, Caro has made many of abstract steel sculptures, often huge and painted in bright colors.

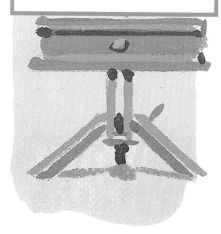

of his sculptures are based on the forms and curves of the female figure. Some of Moore's sculptures are realistic; others are completely abstract shapes. You can see many of Henry Moore's sculptures in natural surroundings in the Yorkshire Sculpture Park, near Leeds, England.

Barbara Hepworth (1903-75) was a friend of Henry Moore and was also influenced by Brancusi. She carved massive abstract shapes in wood and stone, or cast them in bronze. She was influenced by the natural shapes of the landscape and rocks near her home in St. Ives, Cornwall, England.

NEW MATERIALS

During the 20th century, sculptors have experimented with many new materials. Some, such as the artist Andy Warhol, introduced commercial goods like cereal boxes into sculpture. Nicola Hicks uses traditional methods to make sculptures of animals from plaster and straw. Sculptors such as Robert Smithson shape the landscape around them, "sculpting" with earth and other natural materials (see page 80). Others have experimented with plastic, neon tubes, junk materials such as scrap metal, and combinations of materials such as textiles and paint. You can read more about modern-day experiments on pages 80-3.

PHOTOGRAPHY

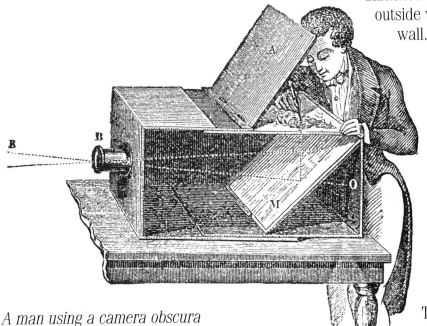

A silhouette picture made in about 1777

TAKING A LIKENESS

People have always liked to own pictures of themselves, but before the days of photography, only artists could produce realistic portraits, and only rich people could afford such pictures. During the 18th century, there was a growing demand for cheaper ways of producing likenesses of people.

Silhouette pictures provided one solution. These pictures were made by tracing around the shadow cast by a lamp and then cutting out the shape in black paper. However, silhouettes had no color or detail. Another solution was the use of the camera obscura. If light shines through a small hole into a darkened room, an image of the world outside will be projected onto the opposite wall. The image is reversed and upside down, but it is clear enough for someone to draw around the outlines. The camera obscura became a useful tool for artists, who traced around the image and used this sketch as the basis for a painting. Portable versions were made, with a glass lens in the hole to give a clearer, brighter image.

A man using a camera obscura to make a sketch

PERMANENT IMAGES

The next question was whether an image could be captured and retained permanently. Scientists already knew that the chemical silver nitrate turns black when it is exposed to light. Various people tried to fix an image on paper with silver salts, but the first person to succeed was the French artist and inventor Joseph Nicéphore Niepce (1765-1833). He used a sheet of paper coated with silver chloride to reproduce the image at the back of a camera obscura.

In 1827, Niepce began to work with another Frenchman, Louis Jacques Mandé Daguerre (1789-1851). In 1835, Daguerre produced an image on a metal plate, known as the "daguerreotype." The quality of daguerreotypes was so good that they were in great demand during the 1840s and 1850s. But the

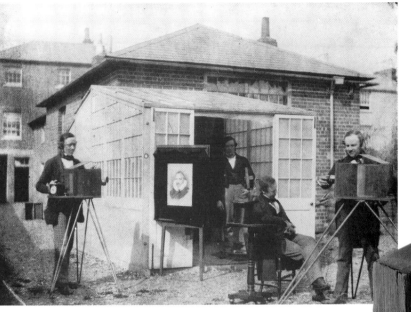

A "positive" paper print made by William Henry Fox Talbot from the negative image below in about 1846.

One of Fox Talbot's early cameras, which his wife called "mousetraps!"

process was complicated and the equipment expensive.

The first person to make a permanent print on paper was a British inventor, William Henry Fox Talbot (1800-77). It took Fox Talbot six years to discover how to convert a negative image into a positive print on paper. However, he eventually established the principle on which modern photography is based—that if transparent paper is used for the first ("negative") image, this can be used to print a second ("positive") image in which the light and dark parts are reversed. Fox Talbot also made some small wooden cameras, which were easy to carry about. His wife called them "mousetraps"!

JULIA MARGARET CAMERON

Portrait photography became fashionable in the 1850s, after the introduction of the wet collodion (also called wet plate) process. This process was messy and difficult, but the quality of the image produced was good. A glass plate was coated with a mixture of chemicals called collodion and then with light-sensitive materials. The glass plate had to be used and developed while it was still wet, so photographers needed a darkroom close by.

One of the best-known portrait photographers of the late 19th century was Julia Margaret Cameron (1815-79). She did not begin to take photographs until she was 48, but she soon became very skilled. She persuaded her friends to sit for portraits and tried to capture their characters in her photographs. She was interested in making her photographs artistic and often composed her pictures in the style of Renaissance paintings.

The Angel at the Sepulcher, *a photographic portrait by Julia Margaret Cameron*

PHOTOGRAPHS OF WAR

Mathew B. Brady (1823-96) was the official photographer of the Civil War (1861-5). With 20 assistants he took over 3,500 images of the war. Brady used the wet collodion process, which meant that it was necessary to have a darkroom near at hand. Brady and his team traveled the battlefields in horse-drawn mobile darkrooms. Never before had war been portrayed in such an immediate way.

The wet collodion process of photography was messy and awkward. Photographers had to carry huge amounts of equipment with them when they traveled, including some kind of darkroom.

PHOTOGRAPHY FOR THE MASSES

A young American bank clerk called George Eastman (1854-1932) tried the wet collodion process but found the equipment messy and cumbersome. Eastman set about inventing a more efficient method of photography. He founded the Eastman Kodak Company (later known simply as Kodak) to carry out his new methods. In 1888, Eastman brought photography to the masses by introducing the Kodak box camera. This camera was loaded with a roll of film instead of plates. When the owner of the camera had finished the roll of film, he or she sent the whole camera back to the Kodak factory where the film was removed and developed. The factory returned the prints, and the camera was reloaded with new film. From then on photographers did not have to set up complicated equipment before taking a picture.

NEW DIRECTIONS

The photograph allowed people to see the world around them in a completely new way. For example, photographs of actual people and places in far-distant lands were far more

CONNECTIONS

Color photographs were first produced by hand-coloring daguerreotypes. Color glass plates were developed by the French inventors, Auguste and Louis Lumière in the early 1900s. But color photography did not become widely available and popular until the 1960s.

"Interior of a Mandarin dwelling, Peking." This is one of the exotic photographs taken by John Thomson on his travels around China in the 1870s.

Migrant Mother, California *by Dorothea Lange*

immediate than any painting. The British photographer John Thomson (1837-1921) traveled around China in the 1870s. On his return to Britain, he published four volumes of photographs called *Illustrations of China and Its People*. Thomson also worked closer to home. His pictures of people on the streets of London were an attempt to bring the plight of the poor to the attention of the wider public. In the 1880s a police reporter called Jacob Riis (1849-1914) photographed people living in the slums in New York. As a result of his pictures, some changes were made to the city's housing laws in an attempt to improve conditions in the slums.

During the 1930s a team of photographers in the United States worked to record the lives of ordinary people across the country. This was a time of great hardship for many people, known as the Depression. One of the photographers, Dorothea Lange (1895-1965), became famous for her stark pictures of starving workers in California. These documentary photographs were reproduced in newspapers and magazines all over the United States, and helped to bring the plight of the workers to the attention of the American public.

PHOTOGRAPHY AND ART

Photography is an art form. Some people think that you just have to "point and snap" and the camera does all the work for you. But the camera

is a tool, just like paint and paintbrush. The photographer must think about composition and lighting, and about shape and texture. Focusing can be sharp or slightly soft to give a more delicate feel to the subject.

One of the most important people to champion the importance of photography as an art was an American called Alfred Stieglitz (1864-1946). He set up a gallery in New York where he exhibited the work of other American photographers, and painters such as Matisse and Picasso. He also showed his own photographs, the most famous of which is *The Steerage*. Stieglitz was married to the painter Georgia O'Keeffe (see page 48).

One of the photographers inspired and encouraged by Stieglitz was Ansel Adams (1902-84). Adams is known best for his black and white photographs of American scenery, particularly the mountainous areas of the western United States, which bring out dramatic lighting contrasts, shapes, and textures.

The Steerage by Alfred Stieglitz. The gangway cuts the picture in half, emphasising the divide between people traveling "steerage" below decks, and those on the upper decks.

HENRI CARTIER-BRESSON

The French photographer Henri Cartier-Bresson (1908-), studied painting before he took up photography in the 1930s. Since then he has traveled all over the world, taking photographs to be published in newspapers, magazines, and books. This kind of photography is known as photojournalism. Cartier-Bresson is the master of what he has called the "decisive moment"—the split-second moment when the photographer presses the camera shutter to capture the most powerful image of an event.

WHAT IS PHOTOGRAPHY?

Photography is the process of capturing and preserving an image to give a permanent picture.

1. Light enters the camera through the lens, a curved circle of glass at the front.
2. As light passes through the lens, the image in front of the camera is projected onto a film inside the camera.
3. The film is covered with a light-sensitive coating that captures the image as a negative (with the light and dark parts reversed).
4. When the film is developed and printed, the image is projected through an enlarger onto light-sensitive paper. The light and dark parts are reversed once again, so that you end up with a positive picture.

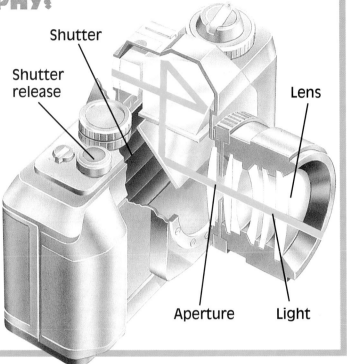

Shutter
Shutter release
Lens
Aperture
Light

INSIDE THE CAMERA

The shutter opens to allow light in when you press the shutter release. If too much light enters the camera, the picture will be "overexposed." If too little light enters, the picture will be "under-exposed." You need to choose the right setting for the conditions. First the shutter speed—this is the time the shutter is open. Second the aperture—this is a circular opening near the shutter. The size of the aperture can also be changed to control the amount of light entering the camera. Photographers use these two settings together. For example, if you wanted to take a picture of a moving car, you would set a very fast shutter speed (perhaps a thousandth of a second) and a wide aperture to allow as much light in as possible for that very brief moment. But for a sunny beach scene, you would set a slower shutter speed and a tiny aperture to prevent too much light from entering.

This shot of a racing car is taken with a very fast shutter speed. The car is in focus, but the background is blurred.

MODERN TECHNIQUES

The photographers of the 19th century would find it hard to believe the changes that have taken place in photography since those early images. Fast films and shutter speeds mean that photographers can take action shots of racing cars, planes, and other moving objects without blurring. Different filters over the lens produce a variety of effects. Multiple images can be created in the darkroom by printing more than one negative onto the same piece of photographic paper. Special "macro" lenses allow photographers to get close in to natural history subjects such as insects.

Many photographers and designers now use computers to manipulate an image taken by a camera. Photographs can be completely rearranged by computer. Using a powerful computer and a photographic package, you can remove unwanted people and objects, move the main subjects around and make them larger so that they fill the frame. Computers can also be used to restore old and damaged photographs. These techniques are useful but the art of photography still relies on the "decisive moment"—getting the perfect shot first time around!

The artist David Hockney has used the camera to create multiple images that he puts together to form a photo collage. My mother, Bradford Yorkshire, 4th May 1982 *is a collage of pictures of Hockney's mother taken from slightly different angles and then put together in a mosaic.*

ART TRENDS

Art trends can be bewildering in their variety. Some artists follow styles similar to those of the past. Many other artists are experimenting with the forms of art, pushing their work to the very limits of what can be called art. To end this journey through the world of art, we will look at just a few of the great variety of artists.

ENVIRONMENTAL SCULPTURE

Robert Smithson (1938-1973) created works, often called *environmental sculpture*, that are actually a part of the world of nature. They include trenches dug in the deserts, as well as rock surfaces. To create his *Spiral Jetty*, Smithson used earth-moving equipment to extend a rock and dirt spiral, 1,500 feet (460 meters) long, into Great Salt Lake in Utah. He explained his scupture this way: "Instead of putting a work of art on some land, some land is put into the work of art."

JUNK SCULPTURE

David Kemp (1945-) uses junk materials that he finds in the landscape around him to create his sculptures. He lives and works in Cornwall, England, and

Junk sculpture by David Kemp. Released Spirits (above), is made from old plastic containers that were washed up on to the beach, and The Wooden Whaler *(right)*

some of his work has been inspired by the ruins of the tin mines that litter the landscape in Cornwall, England. These sculptures make connections with the past history of a place. Others, such as *Released Spirits*, make the viewer look at trash in a completely new way.

INSIDE OUT

Rachel Whiteread's (1963-) sculpture *House* caused a great stir when it first appeared in October 1993. Tens of thousands of people visited the concrete house, which stood in the East End of London.

The house was one of a typical row of Victorian terraced houses. Many of the houses in the row were destroyed during World War II, and more were later demolished to make way for newer styles of housing. By 1993 there was only one house left. Whiteread used this terraced house, which no one lived in, to cast her sculpture.

House *by Rachel Whiteread. A concrete cast of the inside of a real house, the end result looks like an inside-out house.*

To make the sculpture, some things inside the house, such as the stairs, were taken out, and new foundations were laid to carry the weight of the finished work. Then the inside walls of the house were sprayed thickly with concrete. When the concrete had set, the original walls of the house were removed, leaving a cast of the interior. It looked like a big block with the outlines of windows, fireplaces, and other details imprinted in the concrete. Whiteread had turned the house "inside out." *House* stood until January 1994, when it was demolished.

LIFELIKE SCULPTURE

Duane Hanson (1925-) is one of a group of artists who have turned away from abstract art to experiment with a startling realism that involves ordinary subjects. Hanson makes life-size and very lifelike figures out of polyvinyl plastic, fiberglass and

One of Duane Hanson's lifesize and life-like figures, Delivery Man

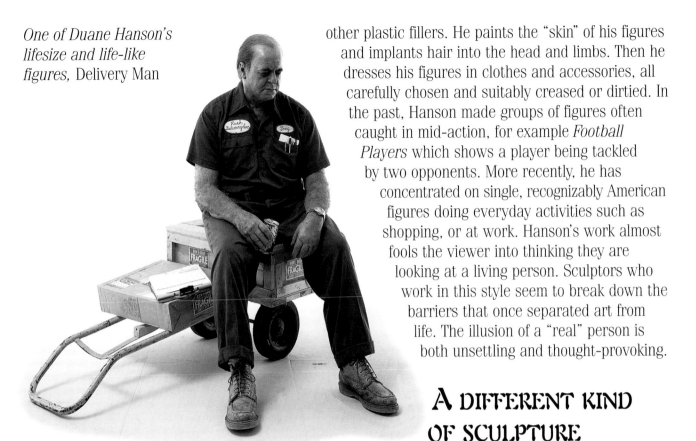

other plastic fillers. He paints the "skin" of his figures and implants hair into the head and limbs. Then he dresses his figures in clothes and accessories, all carefully chosen and suitably creased or dirtied. In the past, Hanson made groups of figures often caught in mid-action, for example *Football Players* which shows a player being tackled by two opponents. More recently, he has concentrated on single, recognizably American figures doing everyday activities such as shopping, or at work. Hanson's work almost fools the viewer into thinking they are looking at a living person. Sculptors who work in this style seem to break down the barriers that once separated art from life. The illusion of a "real" person is both unsettling and thought-provoking.

A DIFFERENT KIND OF SCULPTURE

Damien Hirst (1965-) has become famous for his work using animal carcasses. *The Physical Impossibility of Death in the Mind of Someone Living* (1991) showed a shark carcass in a tank. Another work called *A Thousand Years* was meant to suggest the cycle of life and death.

The Physical Impossibility of Death in the Mind of Someone Living *by Damien Hirst*

Installation art by Simon Patterson

INSTALLATION ART

Douglas Gordon (1966-) uses video installations to try to make people think about their view of the world around them. One of his works uses three sections from a film version of *The Strange Case of Dr. Jekyll and Mr. Hyde* by Robert Louis Stevenson, showing Dr. Jekyll turning into Mr. Hyde. The film is slowed down, and the difference between the man (Dr. Jekyll) and the monster (Mr. Hyde) becomes very unclear. Gordon is also interested in understanding and memory and in 1990 produced his *List of Names*. This was a wall text containing 1,440 names, all of people he had met and could remember while working on the piece.

Simon Patterson (1967-) also uses "installations"—real objects arranged as art. One of his works is three yacht sails mounted on metal stands. Each sail has the name of a famous writer—Raymond Chandler, Currer Bell (Charlotte Brontë), and Laurence Sterne on it. The three names—chandler, bell, and stern—are all also words to do with sailing. Patterson says that the sails are like an artist's blank canvas, and the work is about the problems of making art.

FIND OUT MORE . . .

It is impossible to give a complete picture of what is happening in the art world today, but if you want to find out more, why not go to your local gallery, or watch out for new exhibitions in a nearby town or city? You might see some things that you don't understand or that make you laugh, and you might see some things that inspire you to try out your own ideas at home. Who knows, *you* might be an artist of the future, inspiring coming generations with *your* work.

ART TERMS

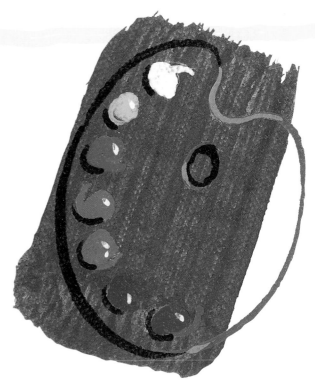

abstract art art that does not represent anything recognizable, but that creates an idea or a mood from colors, or shapes alone.

acrylic a type of paint in which the pigments are mixed with a plastic binder which makes it dry quickly without cracking.

Baroque describes the period in the arts between about 1600 and 1750 characterized by much ornamentation and curved rather than straight lines.

binder in paint, the binder is the liquid part that carries the pigment. The binder helps to spread the pigment evenly, and makes the pigment stick to the surface that is being painted.

chiaroscuro the use of light and shadow in painting.

Classical the period in Greek history which began in about 500 B.C.

collage a composition that is made up of different materials such as fabrics and newsprint, sometimes combined with painting or drawing.

complementary colors colors which are opposite each other on the color wheel and so contrast with each other.

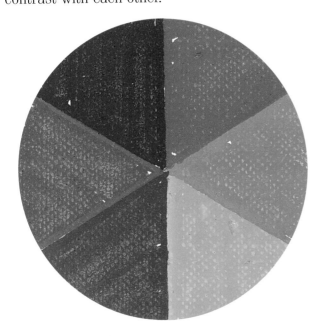

Cubism an art movement developed by Picasso and others in which images are built up using simple lines and angular shapes.

Dada (Dadaism) the name given to an art movement that started as a reaction to World War I (1914-18). Dadaists wanted to express their feelings about the war and the huge waste of life, and they set out to shock the established art world.

daguerreotype an image produced on a metal plate, named after Louis Jacques Mandé Daguerre, and first produced in 1835. The image was clear but very fragile, and had to be enclosed in an airtight glass case to preserve it.

egg tempera a binder made by mixing egg yolk and water which was added to pigments. Egg tempera was used by European artists until the 1400s.

foreshortening a technique of perspective, in which things are painted or drawn as they look in real life. For example, the feet of someone facing forward will be painted to look shorter than the feet of someone facing sideways.

frescoes wall paintings. They are called frescoes because were done while the plaster on the wall was "fresh" (*fresco*), or wet.

Georgian refers to the period in British history when four kings called George reigned one after the other (1714-1830).

gesso plaster of Paris mixed with glue applied to wooden panels to give them a smooth finish for painting on.

Gothic a style of architecture developed in Europe from the 12th century, recognized by its pointed arches.

gouache a thick form of watercolor, made by adding white pigment to the paint. Gouache colors dry more brightly than watercolors.

Impressionism an art movement that began in Paris toward the end of the 19th century. The movement was started by a group of artists led by Édouard Manet. It was named after Claude Monet's painting *Impression: Sunrise* by a critic who mocked the group for the lack of detail in their pictures.

mosaic a design made up of small pieces of colored stone, glass or metals.

Neoclassical an art movement that developed after the discoveries of the Ancient Roman towns of Pompeii and Herculaneum in 1748. This led to a renewed interest in Classical art.

oils paints that use oil (normally linseed) as a binder.

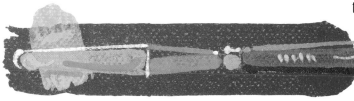

palette knife a blunt blade designed for cleaning paint from an artist's palette or for putting paint on canvas. Some artists paint whole pictures with palette knives, while others use them for putting dollops of paint onto the canvas before spreading it with a brush.

perspective an artistic technique that gives a picture depth. The farther away an object is from you, the smaller it looks. If an artist paints some figures smaller than others, the smaller ones will seem to be further away, even though they are painted on to a flat surface.

pigment in paint, a pigment is the substance that gives the paint its color.

poster paint a thick, brightly colored form of watercolor, often used by children at school.

primary colors the primary colors of paint are red, yellow, and blue.

relief in sculpture, a carving or molding that stands out from a background of stone, metal, or wood.

Rococo an art movement that began in France in the first half of the 18th century. The word *rococo* means "shell-like." Rococo art was elegant and refined.

Romanesque a style of architecture developed in Europe in the 11th century. Romanesque buildings had big round arches like the Roman arches after which the style was named.

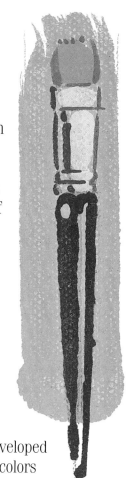

sfumato a style of painting developed by Leonardo da Vinci, in which colors are blended and blurred together so there are no sharp outlines in the picture.

Surrealism an art movement founded in Paris in 1924 by a group of artists that included Salvador Dali, René Magritte, and Joan Miró. Surrealists painted strange, dreamlike pictures. Artists also produced Surrealist sculptures.

terra cotta a brownish-red clay used for pottery and sculpture.

tesselation patterns formed from small squares or cubes (*tesserae*), as in mosaics.

watercolor a type of paint which uses water as a binder.

wet-plate or **wet collodion process** a photographic process in which a glass plate was coated with a mixture of chemicals called collodion, and then with light-sensitive materials. The glass plate had to be used and developed while it was wet, so photographers needed a darkroom close by.

GLOSSARY OF ARTISTS

Adams, Ansel (1902-84) American photographer. Best-known for his stunning black and white photographs of national parks in the United States.

Anguissola, Sofonisba (*c.*1535-1625) Italian painter. Court painter in Madrid. She became internationally famous as a portrait painter.

Arp, Jean Hans (1887-1966) Alsatian painter and sculptor. One of the founders of European Dadaism. First worked in geometric forms then changed to simple rounded images. Joined the Surrealist movement after 1924.

Bacon, Francis (1909-92) British painter. A self-taught artist who began painting in the 1930s. His paintings are often violent, with strong, rich colors and blurred features.

Bernini, Gianlorenzo (1598-1680) Italian sculptor and architect. His architectural works can be seen all over Rome, including his great masterpiece, the piazza in front of St. Peter's.

Bonheur, Rosa (1822-99) French artist. Renowned for her paintings of animals, particularly horses. She was officially granted permission by the French police to wear male dress (trousers) in 1852.

Bosch, Hieronymus (*c.*1450-1516) Dutch painter. Painted weird landscapes full of strange monsters. His paintings were meant to stress the wickedness of people in the medieval world and the evils that would befall them.

Botticelli, Sandro (*c.*1445-1510) Italian painter. One of the greatest artists of the Renaissance in Florence. One of his most famous paintings is *The Birth of Venus*, in which Venus is seen rising from the sea on a shell.

Brancusi, Constantin (1876-1957) Romanian sculptor. He worked in Paris for most of his life. His sculptures, usually in highly polished stone or metal, are abstract shapes.

Braque, Georges (1882-1963) French painter and sculptor. Worked with Picasso to develop Cubism and was one of the first artists to experiment with collage.

Bruegel the Elder, Pieter (*c.* 1525-69) Flemish painter. Was an apprentice in Antwerp before traveling to France and Italy. He painted what he saw around him, whether it was peasants working in the fields or the horrors of war.

Brunelleschi, Filippo (1377-1446) Italian architect and sculptor. He was called one of the "fathers of the Florentine Renaissance." Traveled to Rome with Donatello to study the ruins of ancient buildings and then introduced Classical ideas into his own work.

Calder, Alexander (1898-1976) American sculptor and inventor of mobiles. After completing a degree in engineering, he began to experiment with metal structures, gradually developing them into movable compositions suspended by wire.

Cameron, Julia Margaret (1815-79) British photographer. Followed Classical styles of composition and took many portraits of famous friends, including the poet Alfred Lord Tennyson and the actress Ellen Terry.

Canale, Antonio (Canaletto) (1697-1768) Italian painter. Painted views of Venice, which were particularly popular with English travelers. In 1746 he went to England where he painted views of London.

Canova, Antonio (1757-1822) Italian sculptor. One of the major sculptors of the Neoclassical Age. His work was cold and formal, but his style was greatly admired.

Caravaggio, Michelangelo da (1573-1610) Italian painter. A wild character who refused to conform to artistic ideas of the time. He painted religious characters to look like ordinary people. His painting shocked fashionable society at first, but later became popular.

Caro, Anthony (1924-) British sculptor. Famous for his huge abstract steel sculptures, often painted in bright colors.

Cartier-Bresson, Henri (1908-) French photographer. The pioneer of photojournalism. His photographs provide a record of world events but often capture the fleeting emotions and reactions of ordinary people.

Cassatt, Mary (1844-1926) American painter. Worked mainly in Paris where she exhibited with the Impressionists and became a close friend of Edgar Degas.

Cézanne, Paul (1839-1906) French painter. He began to paint with the Impressionists but wanted to develop a more vibrant style that captured the bright colors of southern France. He is sometimes called the "father of modern art" because his work led the way to later styles.

Chagall, Marc (1887-1985) Russian painter. He spent most of his life in France but used his childhood experiences in Russia to paint pictures that are almost like folk art.

Cimabue (*c*.1240-1302) Italian painter. With Giotto he revived fresco painting.

Claude Lorrain (1600-82) French painter. Worked in Italy, studying the countryside around Rome for his landscapes. His paintings are in the Classical style, with beautiful dreamlike scenery and images from mythology.

Constable, John (1776-1837) English painter. He painted landscapes and influenced the French Barbizon group. He painted landscapes as he saw them, with rain and cloudy skies, often putting colors on with a palette knife.

Corot, Jean Baptiste Camille (1796-1875) French painter. A member of the Barbizon Group, he painted landscapes and portraits, concentrating on tones rather than color. His soft landscapes were very popular during his lifetime.

Courbet, Gustave (1819-77) French painter. He protested against the Classical school of painting and painted natural subjects, showing hardship and poverty where he saw it.

Dali, Salvador (1904-89) Spanish painter. A leading artist of the Surrealist movement. He painted objects that did not go together, or did not look as they should, to create a nightmare quality in his work.

David, Jacques-Louis (1748-1825) French painter. He supported the revolutionaries during the French Revolution and became their official painter. After the Revolution he became Napoleon's court painter.

Degas, Edgar (1834-1917) French painter. One of the Impressionists who was trained under Ingres. Unlike the other Impressionists, he preferred painting indoor scenes, and many of his works show ballerinas rehearsing or performing.

de Kooning, Willem (1904-97) Dutch-American painter. Member of Abstract Expressionist group with Jackson Pollock, although he often portrayed the human figure in his paintings.

Delacroix, Eugène (1798-1863) French painter. A leader of the Romantic Movement in France. He had no patience with people who imitated the Classical artists and believed that color was more important than precise drawing.

Delaunay, Robert (1885-1941) French painter. He tried to turn Cubism away from drab browns and grays and painted in bright, hectic colors.

Donatello (*c*. 1386-1466) Italian sculptor. The finest of the sculptors working in Florence during the Renaissance. He worked in wood, stone, and bronze and sculpted his figures by observing people in real life.

Duchamp, Marcel (1887-1968) French painter. Started the Dadaist Movement in New York. His work shocked the American public when it was exhibited there.

Dürer, Albrecht (1471-1528) German painter and engraver. Traveled to Italy to learn about the Renaissance artists and then introduced Renaissance ideas into northern Europe. His finest works are engravings and woodcuts.

El Greco ("the Greek") (1541-1614) Spanish painter, born on the Greek island of Crete. Studied under Titian in Venice and was greatly influenced by Tintoretto. His distinctive paintings show people with pale faces and elongated limbs.

Eyck, Jan van (*c*.1390-1441) Flemish painter. One of the leading artists of the Renaissance in northern Europe. Developed the technique of painting in oils rather than egg tempera.

Fontana, Lavinia (1552-1614) Italian painter. She became official painter at the papal court in Rome and conducted successful workshops in Rome and Bologna.

Francesca, Piero della (c.1420-92) Italian painter. An early Renaissance artist, he painted frescoes using perspective and color and light to portray solid forms.

Frankenthaler, Helen (1928-) American painter. She has developed a distinctive method of staining untreated canvases and using thin washes of color to create a floating effect.

Freud, Lucian (1922-) British painter. One of the most notable painters at work today, with a particular talent for painting nudes that look like real people, with all their faults.

Frink, Elisabeth (1930-93) British sculptor. Had a particular interest in sculpting human heads and figures.

Gainsborough, Thomas (1727-88) English painter. A rival of Sir Joshua Reynolds as a portrait painter of fashionable society. He had a talent for painting shimmering fabrics.

Gauguin, Paul (1848-1903) French painter. Gave up work as a stockbroker to paint with the Impressionists. Went to Tahiti, an island in the Pacific Ocean, where he painted the colorful, exotic scenes around him.

Gentileschi, Artemisia (1593-c. 1652) Italian painter. She was influenced by Caravaggio's dramatic style and painted portraits of many famous women in history including Mary Magdalene and Lucretia.

Ghiberti, Lorenzo (1378-1455) Italian sculptor. Working at the same time as Brunelleschi in the early Renaissance. Between 1424 and 1452, he sculpted a pair of bronze church doors that Michelangelo described as "The Gates of Paradise."

Ghirlandaio, Domenico (1449-94) Italian painter. One of the leading masters of the 15th century, who trained Michelangelo for three years. He painted religious subjects as though they were happening in Florence at the time.

Gilbert (1943-) and **George** (1942-) British

sculptors. Met at St Martin's College of Art and decided to change contemporary trends by becoming "living sculptures." Have exhibited worldwide since 1969.

Giotto di Bondone (c.1266-1337) Italian painter. With Cimabue, he revived the art of painting frescoes but broke away from the formal style of the past, and made his people and scenes look more realistic.

Gogh, Vincent van (1853-90). Dutch painter. Met Impressionist painters in Paris in 1886. Developed a personal style using bright colors laid thickly on the canvas.

Gordon, Douglas (1966-) British painter and installation artist. Uses painting, installation, and film to explore memory and the meaning of life's experiences.

Gorky, Arshile (1904-48) Armenian painter. Went to the United States in 1920 to study art. Early works show influence of Picasso, but he was later influenced by Surrealism and Abstract Expressionism.

Goya, Francisco de (1746-1828) Spanish painter. Court painter to the Spanish king, Charles IV. He painted the royal family and dramatic war pictures showing the brutality of Napoleon's troops towards the Spaniards.

Hepworth, Barbara (1903-75) British sculptor. A friend of Henry Moore, was influenced by Brancusi and Arp. She created massive abstract sculptures in wood, stone, and metal.

Hirst, Damien (1965-) British sculptor and painter. Aims to make "art that everybody could believe in," and much of his work deals with aspects of life and death.

Hockney, David (1937-) British painter. Traveled in the United States where he developed his style of painting, portraying the world around him with realism and wit.

Holbein the Younger, Hans (*c.* 1497-1543) German painter and engraver. After the Reformation, went to London where he established himself as a portrait painter. Became court painter to King Henry VIII.

Homer, Winslow (1836-1910) American painter. Was an illustrator for the magazine *Harper's Weekly* and was its artistic correspondent during the Civil War.

Ingres, Jean Auguste Dominique (1780-1867) French painter. Was a student of Jacques Louis David. He admired the Classical art of the ancients and the Renaissance painters. Many people at the time found his art cold and perfect.

Kandinsky, Wassily (1866-1944) Russian painter. One of the first artists to paint completely abstract works and a founding member of the German "Blue Rider" group which stressed color and shape rather than subject.

Kemp, David (1945-) British sculptor. Works with scrap materials and debris, often relating his sculptures to the history of their surroundings.

Klee, Paul (1879-1940) German-Swiss painter. Was impressed by Cubist experiments and set out to find new ways of creating images. Combined lines, shades and colors to create real or weird and fantastic subjects.

Krasner, Lee (1908-84) American painter. Married to Jackson Pollock and experimented with similar abstract painting.

Lange, Dorothea (1895-1965) American photographer. Originally a society photographer, she decided to photograph the misery of poverty caused by the Depression in 1930s. Her photographs helped to raise awareness of the suffering in the western United States.

Lawrence, Jacob (1917-) American painter. Influenced by Orozco and Rivera, Lawrence paints the daily lives and history of black people in the United States.

Leonardo da Vinci (1452-1519) Italian painter. One of the finest painters of the Italian Renaissance. He was also a scientist and inventor. Developed the technique of *sfumato* in his paintings.

Lichtenstein, Roy (1923-) American painter and sculptor. Best known for using a dot technique to create color and shading that looks like the illustrations in comics.

Magritte, René (1898-1967) Belgian painter. A Surrealist artist who painted dreamlike images that look real and are painted accurately but that are almost impossible to explain.

Manet, Édouard (1832-83) French painter. The leader of the group of artists known as the Impressionists. His paintings show the harsh effects of sunlight, with people's faces flattened by bright light.

Masaccio (1401-28) Italian painter. The first 15th-century master in Florence. He was the first painter to use the principles of perspective introduced by Brunelleschi.

Matisse, Henri (1869-1954) French painter and sculptor. The most famous of the artists who called themselves *Les Fauves* (the wild beasts). He painted very decorative pictures using patterns and bold contrasting colors.

Michelangelo Buonarroti (1475-1564) Italian painter and sculptor. One of the most famous of the Renaissance artists. He thought of himself as a sculptor, but one of his best-known works is the magnificent painted ceiling of the Sistine Chapel in Rome.

Millet, Jean François (1814-75) French painter. His landscapes showed the realities of country life, with peasants at work in the fields.

Miró, Joan (1893-1983) Spanish painter. One of the Surrealist group, though his paintings are almost abstract. He used bright primary colors and curved lines to create Surrealist images.

Modigliani, Amedeo (1884-1920) Italian painter and sculptor. He met Brancusi in Paris who introduced him to African art. The heads he sculpted were inspired by African masks.

Mondrian, Piet (1872-1944) Dutch painter. Experimented with a development of abstract art and Cubism—paintings made up entirely of straight lines and colors, which he felt were the perfect harmony of color and shape.

Monet, Claude (1840-1926) French painter. A leading member of the Impressionist group, who painted the picture that gave the movement its name.

Moore, Henry (1898-1986) British sculptor and painter. One of the greatest artists of the 20th century. He is best known for his large sculptures of the female form, some realistic and some abstract.

Morisot, Berthe (1841-95) French painter. Married to Manet's brother, Eugene. Encouraged by Corot and inspired by him to paint outdoors. She painted with bright colors and loose, expressive brushstrokes.

Morris, William (1834-96) British painter and designer. He did not like the new industrial methods of the time and founded a firm to produce furniture, wallpaper, carpets, tapestries, and stained-glass windows, which he designed.

Munch, Edvard (1863-1944) Norwegian painter. Spent time in Paris and Berlin. His main influence was Gauguin. He later depicted loneliness, despair, fear, and death in paintings such as *The Scream*.

Nevelson, Louise (1900-1988) Russian-born American sculptor. Assembled machine-made wooden objects into extraordinary sculptures with compartments that seem to open into or suggest eternity.

O'Keeffe, Georgia (1887-1986) American painter. Though best known for her closeups of flower heads, she later took inspiration from the open spaces of New Mexico, painting the landscapes and architecture of the region.

Orozco, José Clemente (1883-1949) Mexican painter. He is most famous for his frescoes, which often have a political theme.

Picasso, Pablo (1881-1973) Spanish painter and sculptor. He developed Cubism, in which images are built up using lines and angular shapes.

Pollock, Jackson (1912-56) American painter. A leading figure in the Abstract Expressionist movement. He created his paintings by laying the canvas on the floor and dripping or pouring paint onto it to form a jumble of lines and colors.

Poussin, Nicolas (1594-1665) French painter. Studied Titian's paintings and used the same movement and glowing colors in his own landscapes and figure paintings.

Raphael (Raffaello Santi) (1483-1520) Italian painter. With Leonardo da Vinci and Michelangelo, one of the leading Renaissance painters. His figures have a serene beauty, and his compositions are perfectly balanced.

Rauschenberg, Robert (1925-) American painter. Famous for experimenting with various materials, techniques, and styles, such as combining printmaking techniques with painting and drawing.

Rembrandt van Rijn (1606-69) Dutch painter. One of the great portrait painters.

Renoir, Pierre Auguste (1841-1919) French painter. An Impressionist artist who liked to paint crowds of people enjoying themselves, showing the gaiety of the people but also the bright colors of the scene.

Reynolds, Sir Joshua (1723-92) British painter. A portrait painter in fashionable London society, he founded the Royal Academy of Art. He painted in a more Classical style than his rival, Thomas Gainsborough.

Riis, Jacob (1849-1914) Danish-born American photographer. A police reporter who became well-known for his gritty photographs of life in the New York slums.

Riley, Bridget (1931-) British painter. Had her first solo exhibition in 1962. Creates three-dimensional effects by the use of color and geometric patterns and lines.

Rivera, Diego (1886-1957) Mexican painter. Painted frescoes showing scenes from Mexican history, including the Aztec and Mayan civilizations and political events.

Rodin, Auguste (1840-1917) French sculptor. One of the greatest sculptors of his time. Some of his most famous works are *The Kiss*, *The Thinker* and *The Hand of God*.

Rothko, Mark (1903-70) Russian painter. An Abstract Expressionist who emigrated to the United States in 1913. The mood of his paintings is conveyed by simple oblongs of hazy color on mural-sized canvases.

Rousseau, Henri (1844-1910) French painter. Painted pictures with clear lines and pure colors. This style inspired other artists to turn away from complicated experiments and paint from their own experience.

Rubens, Peter Paul (1577-1640) Flemish painter. Considered to be one of the most talented painters of his day. He had a particular talent for painting flesh tones and large, complicated works.

Ruysch, Rachel (1664-1750) Dutch painter. Specialist in flower painting, she was able to charge high prices for her detailed paintings.

Seurat, Georges (1859-91) French painter. Combined studies of the science of color with Impressionist ideas to develop his own style, known as Pointillism. His paintings are composed of tiny dots and simple shapes.

Smithson, Robert (1938-1973) American sculptor. Created works known as environmental sculpture.

Stieglitz, Alfred (1864-1946) American photographer. Promoted the idea of photography as an art form. He exhibited the works of American photographers and artists such as Matisse at his gallery in New York.

Thomson, John (1837-1921) British photographer. Well-known for his photographs of people and places, including China and the streets of London.

Tintoretto, Jacopo (1518-94) Italian painter. Worked in Venice and was a pupil of Titian. Made his paintings dramatic by using strange light and sometimes weird figures flying through the air.

Titian, Vecelli (*c.* 1488-1576) Italian painter. Worked in Venice. He painted exuberant mythological subjects such as *The Triumph of Bacchus and Ariadne*. His works became famous for their rich colors and variety of tones.

Turner, Joseph Mallord (1775-1851) English painter. Used light and dramatic color rather than solid shapes. His work influenced the French Impressionist artists.

Velázquez, Diego (1599-1660) Spanish painter. Court painter to King Philip IV of Spain. He studied Caravaggio's work and made use of light and color to bring his portraits to life.

Vermeer, Jan (1632-75) Dutch painter. He painted interiors and was a great master of light and color. His paintings often show people carrying out simple, everyday tasks.

Vigée-Lebrun, Marie-Louise Élisabeth (1755-1842) French painter. Forced to flee France during the French Revolution. She traveled around Europe, achieving great success as a portrait artist.

Warhol, Andy (*c.* 1928-87) American painter. He was a Pop artist, who painted subjects such as soup cans and portraits of film stars.

Whistler, James Abbott McNeill (1834-1903) American painter. Went to Paris where he worked with the Impressionists. He was not strictly an Impressionist, because he was more interested in composing delicate figure-studies than in the effects of light.

Whiteread, Rachel (1963-) British sculptor. Attracted wide attention in 1990 for her sculpture *Ghost*, a white plaster cast of a whole room. *House*, a cast of the inside of a London house, won the Turner Prize in 1993.

INDEX